RON MANGUS' CUSTOM HOT ROD INTERIORS SERIES

FORD ROADSTER
CUSTOM INTERIORS

RON MANGUS
AND
GARY D. SMITH

California Bill's
Automotive Handbooks

Publishers
Howard W. Fisher
Helen V. Fisher

Editor
Howard W. Fisher

Cover and Interior Design
Gary D. Smith, Performance Design
www.performancedesign.net

Cover and Interior Photography
Gary D. Smith, Performance Design
Pages 152–159, Shelley Bernd,
www.HotRodHappenings.com

Copyright © 2008 by Ron Mangus and
Gary D. Smith.

Published by
California Bill's Automotive Handbooks
P.O. Box 91858
Tucson, AZ 85752-1858
520-547-2462
www.californiabills.com

Distributed to bookstores by
Motorbooks International
729 Prospect Avenue
P.O. Box 1
Osceola, WI 54020-0001

ISBN-10 1-931128-26-X
ISBN-13 978-1-931128-26-1

Printed in China

1 2 3 4 5 6 7 8 9 14 13 12 11 10 09 08

All rights reserved. No part of this book may be reproduced or transmitted in any form or by any means, electronic or mechanical, including photocopy, recording or any information storage and retrieval system, without written permission from the publisher, except by a reviewer who may quote brief passages in a review.

Notice: This information in this book is true and complete to the best of our knowledge. It is offered without guarantees on the part of the author or California Bill's Automotive Handbooks. The author(s) and publisher disclaim all liability in connection with the use of this book.

Contents

About the Authors — 6
Introduction — 7
Ron's Shop — 8
Ron's Hot Rods — 10
Hot Rodding History — 12
Ron's Customers — 14

The Cars

Larry Murray's '32 Ford — 16
Jim St. Martin's '32 Ford — 24
Bruce McDowell's '29 Ford — 32
Danny Santoro's '32 Ford — 40
Lee Marquez's '32 Ford — 48
Nathan Tuttle's '32 Ford — 56
Matt Tachdjian's '32 Ford Muroc — 64
Lenn Pritchard's '32 Ford — 72
Marv Anders' '34 Ford — 80
SO-CAL's '32 Ford — 88
George Johnson's '32 Ford — 96
Richard Seals' '35 Ford — 104
Bob Gory's '33 Ford — 112
Jack Bockelman's '33 Ford Speedstar — 120
Ken Sapper's '32 Ford — 128
Chick Koszis' '32 Ford — 136
Fred Fleet's '32 Ford — 144
Mac Bernd's '32 Ford — 152

About the Authors

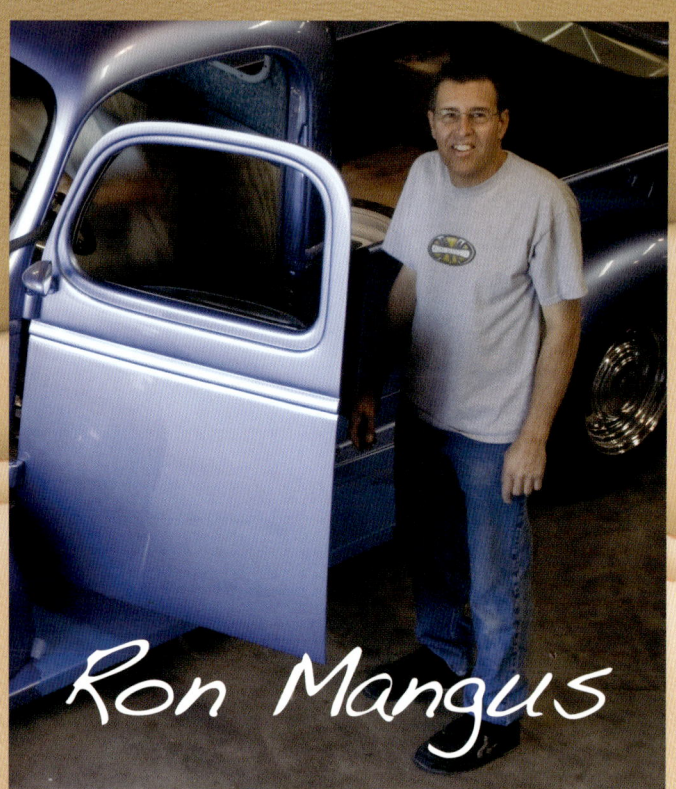

Ron Mangus

Ron started his stitching career in 1969 under the tutelage of his brother Ernie Yanez. Ernie provided special efforts over the course of twenty years in getting Ron started on the right track. Ron credits his brother for teaching him the auto upholstery craft and business, and providing a foundation for the reputation he enjoys today.

In 1989 Ron opened his own shop, Custom Auto Interiors, in Bloomington, California. During this era he also taught basic and advanced upholstery classes at San Bernardino Valley College for four years. Students who were talented enough to take his advanced course learned Ron's techniques for sculpting foam, creating molded headliners, and building custom door panels.

Soon after opening his own shop, a roadster with his interior won America's Most Beautiful Roadster at the 1992 Oakland Roadster Show. Ron's work has since received numerous Best Interior Awards at a variety of car shows.

Ron "The Stitcher" has become famous as a creator of fabulous interiors. From the 1990s through today street rod and hot rodding magazines have featured spectacular cars that show off his interiors.

Photo by Daniel B. Smith

Gary D. Smith

The Riverside International Raceway in Riverside, California, is now a shopping center. But when Gary was a teenager, it was one of the premier road racing tracks in the country. When the Can-Am and Trans-Am came to town, Gary could be found at the Raceway, taking photos. Interest in cars lead to modifying his own street cars and local club drag racing. He crewed on a SCCA Trans-Am Corvette in the mid '70s.

Gary was also interested in car design. He competed in the General Motor's Fisher Body Craftsman's Guild model car design contest, and in 1969 enrolled at the Art Center College of Design in Los Angeles, California. After graduating in 1973 with a degree in Industrial/Transportation design, he was recruited by General Motors Design Staff at the General Motors Technical Center in Warren, Michigan. He worked there as a Senior Creative Designer in Pontiac, Buick, Oldsmobile, and Cadillac exterior design studios. He is responsible for the exterior styling of the Oldsmobile Concept car that lead to the 1992 Oldsmobile Achieva SCX coupe.

In 1988, Gary and his family moved to Arizona, and Gary started Performance Design, freelancing as an industrial/graphic designer and illustrator. Gary also became proficient in desktop publishing and computer graphics. He has been involved with many businesses as an art-director level designer and consultant. In 1996, Gary was introduced to "California Bill" Fisher. Through the relationship that has continued with Bill's son Howard, Gary has been involved in the creation of many automotive titles published by California Bill's Automotive Handbooks.

How-to articles and finished car features showing Mangus' techniques and expertise have appeared in *Hot Rod, Rod & Custom, Street Rodder, Truckin', American Rodder, The Rodder's Journal*, and many more. Special cars with interiors created by Ron and his team include CheZoom and Aluma-Coupe of Boyd's Hot Rods, Billy "ZZ Top" Gibbons' Kopperhed, along with cars for Tim Allen, Pete Chapouris of SO-CAL Speed Shop, Linda Vaughn (Miss Hurst), Thom Taylor, Bruce Meyer, Kenny Bernstein, Robby Gordon, Sammy Hagar, Michael Anthony, Cory McClenathan, and James Brubaker of Universal Studios.

In 2000 Ron was asked to help create a special car for builder Randy Clark from Hot Rods and Custom Stuff of Escondido, California. Their 1949 Chevy Business Coupe won the coveted Ridler award at the Detroit Autorama in 2001. This car was featured on the cover of *Super Rod* in April/May, 2001. This car also won the prestigious "Yosemite" Sam Radoff Sculptural Excellence Award that recognizes both the interior and the entire concept of a car. Ron felt a great accomplishment in achieving these awards.

The 2005 Grand National Roadster Show Best Interior Award went to a 1968 Camaro convertible again upholstered by Ron and built by Randy Clark of Hot Rods and Custom Stuff.

Ron's striking two-tone interior was featured in Richard Tapia's '70 Chevelle winning the 2006 Houston AutoRama's Best of Show as well as Best Interior. This car also won Best of Show at Super Chevy in Pomona, and numerous top awards at the Grand National Roadster Show.

Eventually hot rodders knew Ron's work and reputation by name. So, in 2006, the original shop, Custom Auto Interiors, was renamed Ron Mangus Hot Rod Interiors.

Recently the 2008 Grand National Roadster Best Interior Award went to Ron's creation of Janice Groesbeck's 1956 Chevy convertible.

While Ron is at the highest levels of automotive design and creation, his best work may be yet to come.

Introduction

I hope you will find my passion and love for these cars in the photographs throughout the book.

What drives my passion? Where do I get the inspiration and vision for each project? Those questions have been asked of me a lot more frequently than you might imagine.

What people tell me is that when a car arrives here, I look at the car and learn about the person who owns the car and try to individualize it to his or her needs and ideas. As a result, every interior ends up with a unique design. I take each car under my wing and treat it like it's my own car and, unfortunately, I have to give it back when I'm done. I show that passion to my customers, and they sense that when they come in. They feel welcome and, when the job is complete, they know that I have given them the best job with the highest craftsmanship possible.

As you are looking through the photos in this book you will find that, although there may be similarities in approach, each car is completed with its own special characteristics.

Ron Mangus

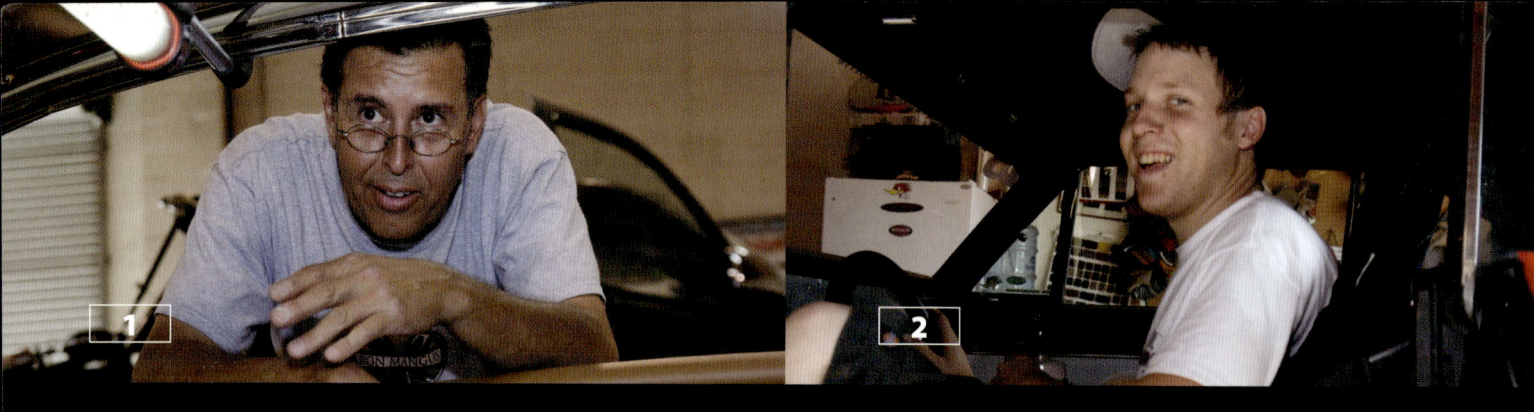

Ron's Shop

Ron Mangus Custom Hot Rod Interiors is a fast-paced business with tight deadlines. In spite of the rush, Ron pays attention to every detail, with no compromises when it comes to quality, craftsmanship, and design. His hand-picked, dedicated team works together seamlessly, creating the many subassemblies that make up a car's interior. He involves his customers in the design process, discussing the design, material selection, and helps them visualize his ideas on how to blend his customer's desires with the car's character to create a masterpiece.

1
Last minute details are addressed as a 1955 Chevy Bel Air is completed.

2
Ron's son, Ryan, is an important part of the business, and is fast becoming a rising interior design star in his own right.

3
A great friend, Pete Salas has worked with Ron for more than 25 years.

4
Ron is proud of his team for their dedication to quality and craftsmanship. They share Ron's design philosophy, treating every car as if it was their own.

Ron's personal attention to his customers builds long-term relationships, referrals, and repeat business. His "hands-on" involvement with every aspect of the design ensures originality and quality.

Ron's Hot Rods

1
"This '56 Ford pickup was my daily driver for 15 years. It's been in the family since it was purchased new and my son Ryan now has it. It was originally used on my father-in-law's chicken ranch."

2
"My '37 Ford Tudor Sedan broke new ground with a two-tone interior that matched the exterior. It was featured in the *American Rodder Collector Special Edition*, September 1996."

3
"I built this '32 from a Total Cost Involved chassis in 1997. It was painted in gelcoat so I could really enjoy driving the car. I could do a burn out and just plow through puddles. This was my rat rod before they reached their current popularity. It was a great car."

4
"I think I was the first to do a flame billet steering wheel. I should have patented the design!"

5
Ron's T-Roadster, taken in 1988. "The car was fast. It would shift out of low at 65 mph. I had to drive slowly over bumps and approach driveways at an angle because the oil plug was really low, and I didn't want to knock it off. The whole family would crowd into the car to go to cruise night. Ryan and I got caught in the rain more than once. We had a lot of fun with that car."

6
"Having always had a passion for motorcycles I began riding again about eight years ago. Being childhood friends with award winning motorcycle builder Jerry Covington (Covington's Cycle City, Woodward, Oklahoma) allowed me to use one of his rolling chassis. Another friend Dean Padie built this bike."

Hot Rodding History

1
This '32 Ford roadster was originally built in 1978 by Barry Lobeck. The 1994 restoration was upholstered by Ron Mangus. *Street Rodder* magazine, March 1995. The Bruce Meyer Collection.

2
Bob Rosenthal's 1936 Ford was first place winner in the 1935–1948 Custom Rod Roadster class at the 2007 Grand National Roadster Show with Ron's interior. *The Rodder's Journal* #34.

3
The "M-80," a '49 Chevy Business Coupe owned by Chris Williams won the Ridler Award in 2001 with upholstery by Ron Mangus. *Super Rod*, April 2001.

4
In the early '60s Dick Bergren made this classic '50s hot rod into one of the most admired and well-proportioned, chopped three window coupes ever. Known as the Doyle Gammell Coupe, it was featured in *Rod and Custom* magazine, December 1963. Bruce Meyer owns the car, and Ron restored the interior to original. *The Rodder's Journal* #29.

5
SO-CAL's Alex Xydias, founder of SO-CAL Speed Shop, came to Ron to upholster the seat for the restored Belly Tank racer that ran 198 mph at Bonneville in 1952. Ron also upholstered the traditional interior for the SO-CAL '32 Hi-boy that started a revolution in hot rodding in the '90s.

6
Here is an integral part of hot rodding history. This is the original chopped top Merc by Sam Barris. This car was recently restored by Roy Brizio Street Rods and is owned by John Mumford. Ron felt honored to help complete this period-correct restoration. *The Rodder's Journal* #38.

Ron Mangus' Custom Hot Rod Interiors • 13

Ron's Customers

1
Tim Allen's 1946 Ford, from the TV show Tool Time. The Ford features distressed leather in '40s–'50s style by Ron Mangus. *Rod & Custom* magazine, April 1999.

2
Jeremy McGrath, the original extreme athlete, made motor sports history with his high-flying freestyle motocross antics. A hot rodder at heart, he went to Ron Mangus to have his '33 Ford upholstered. Built by Dominator Motor Sport Fabrication, Brentwood, California, it won Most Elegant Rod at the inaugural Oakland Rod, Custom, and Motorcycle Show in 2001. *Street Rodder* magazine, September 2003.

3
A 1950 Ford business coupe one-off show car? Ford never made one. Enter Billy "ZZ Top" Gibbons who envisioned the transformation and Pete Chapouris who made it happen. Ron Mangus duplicated the 2-inch Tijuana style tuck 'n roll from 20-year-old copper vinyl surrounded by bright white. *Hot Rod* magazine, January 1996.

4
Bob Stewart, son of hot rod hero Ed "Axle" Stewart, owns this 1932 Ford. This roadster was built in the 1940s and saw quite a bit of dry lakes action from 1947–1949 and clocked a speed of 128.93 mph on July 18, 1948 at El Mirage. Period interior by Ron Mangus.

5
Rock star singer Sammy Hagar with his buggy in Cabo. Interior by Ron Mangus.

6
Larry Erickson's Aluma-Coupe, built by Boyd Coddington, gave Ron a chance to work with the talented team at Boyd's Hot Rod Shop. This interior was completed without using a single stitch. The sculpted interior was all molded and carefully glued in place.

3

WHAT'S HOT FOR '96

Kopperhed is powered by an overhead—like a .030-inch-over '57 Y-block cooled by a U.S. Radiator, fitted with a three-pot Offy intake sporting Ford carbs, repop air cleaners and detailed cast finned-aluminum rocker covers. F-600 truck exhaust manifolds were ground smooth and sprayed with a high-temp coating.

PC3g wheels—actually 16-inch '49 Ford centers offset-welded by Pete Eastwood to custom-rolled 16x7 rims—support four BFGoodrich P205/55ZR16 radials augmented by Coker-supplied Atlas add-on whitewalls. Presto, radial whites.

KOPPERHED

By Gray Baskerville

Let's pretend that 45 years ago Ford commissioned an artist/designer, such as Steve Stanford, to draw a one-off concept car based on a '50 Ford single-bench-seat business coupe. Let's fast-forward to 1956, when the concept coupe, a three-window precursor to the '55 T-bird, has outlived its usefulness and been sold to a second owner. Luck would have it that the new owner was your middle-of-the-road hot rodder—too lean to do a full custom but fat enough to afford an engine swap and a few other low-buck mods, such as heated front coils, a pair of 4-inch lowering blocks, twin pipes, add-on whites and a "Tijuana" trim job.

That is what Billy "ZZ Top" Gibbons envisioned when he commissioned Pete Chapouris' PC3g (aka re-Pete & Jake's) to create what he calls "Kopperhed." As with many similar rod-related projects that went from hibernation to hypersonic, Kopperhed began as a practical daily-driver upgrade—after Billy had bought an Uncle Daniel one-owner '50 from one of Chapouris and Bob Bauder's clients. Then it soon took on a life of its own—a twist here, a turn there as Reverend Billy's imaginative inclinations ultimately transformed this mundane business coupe into

Photography: Jim Brown/PPC Photographic & Gray Baskerville

Chrome rear-fender beads were a stock option that had to be straightened by Jim "Jake" Jacobs. The only alteration to the stock rear bumper was the removal of the guards.

Ronnie Mangus (and crew) duplicated the 2-inch Tijuana-style seats and door panels with bright white vinyl. The copper insert was made from original 20-year-old material that was obtained from S&S in Oregon. The balance of K-hed's interior elements include custom-shaped, engine-turned step plates, a J.B. Donaldson-restored Crest Liner steering wheel, a Jake-modified dash (to accept the stereo tuner) and a T-Bird-shaped frame. The instruments are original, but the knobs were made by PC3g.

4

5

6

LARRY MURRAY'S
'32 Ford

If you appreciate traditional, old school hot rods, you'll really like Larry's '32 basic no frills Hi-boy Ford roadster. It has a 291 cubic inch "FireDome" hemi from a 1955 DeSoto, and early speed equipment including 294 Stromberg carburetors, Edmunds intake manifold, and a Mallory YC dual-point distributor. The 16-inch painted Ford steel wheels are mounted on Buick drum brakes, supported by a Super Bell dropped front axle in the front, and a straight axle with a Ford 9-inch rear end in the back. The interior features an instrument panel, steering column, and steering wheel from a '40 Ford. And the semi-flat black paint says hot rod like no other color.

Larry bought the car basically as you see it here. The car was completed in 2006.

However, the '32 didn't have much of an interior, so he took the car to Ron for his creative touches, and Ron created a traditional 1½" tuck 'n roll maroon leather interior. The fit and finish is outstanding with great attention to detail, as evidenced by the traditional tailored storage pockets in the doors.

Larry first met Ron with Boyd Coddington at Ron's shop in the '80s, and Ron has upholstered nine cars for Larry over the years, including several 1940 Fords.

Body: All steel by Brookville Roadster, Inc., Brookville, Ohio
Chassis: Pete & Jake's, Peculiar, Missouri
Engine: 291 DeSoto hemi
Drivetrain: GM Turbo Hydramatic 400, 9-inch Ford rear end
Wheels: 16-inch Ford steel wheels
Tires: Firestone, front: 5.60"×16", rear: 7.00"×16"

Ron Mangus' Custom Hot Rod Interiors • 17

Larry's '32 Ford has many old school period correct details, like the '40 Ford dash, steering wheel, and shifter. Ron knew instinctively what needed to be done to the interior to retain the authentic, old school look of the car. Tuck 'n roll maroon leather, door pockets, and straight design elements fit the car perfectly. The '40 Ford instrument panel makes the car look as if it was hot rodded in the '40s.

1
Straight lines and French stitching make for a simple, straight-forward design with a functional, nostalgic feel. Notice the symmetry of the repeated widths between the edges of the door panels and the vertical stitching. The seat has a modest thigh bolster that helps hold occupants in the seats.

2
Black loop carpet brings the black exterior color over the instrument panel and onto the floor of the car, and goes great with the maroon leather.

3
Tailored door pockets with French stitching add both a period styling clue and practical storage to the car's interior. It has an art deco luggage feel about it.

4
Notice the controlled surfacing around the door latch. Small details like this one add up to make a tremendous difference in the overall presentation of the interior.

5
Larry's '32 has original style interior door handles with chrome bezels.

Ron Mangus' Custom Hot Rod Interiors • 21

1
Close-up of storage pocket door, vertical seams, and French stitching.

2
1½" tuck 'n roll pleats carry the vertically stitched door design into the seating surfaces.

3
Design symmetry in the doors and seats convey '30s originality. The doors have original style leather check straps.

4
The door theme is carried into the kick panels, including one vertical seam.

5
The straight forward design of the interior is carried into the trunk, with a single line of French stitching, black loop carpet, and a leather covered battery box.

6
The '40 Ford instrument cluster's chrome trim, wood grain insert, and speedometer graphics are fun to look at and a throw back to a much more simple era.

7
Tightly controlled tuck 'n roll pleats in the seat line up perfectly with the seat back.

8
The car is rich with period-correct details.

Jim St. Martin's
'32 Ford

Jim's '32 started with a TCI chassis from a '32 Tudor sedan. After purchasing the chassis, Jim realized that he'd have to pinch and stretch the frame to accommodate the traditional Hi-Boy roadster that he wanted to build. He found a Brizio chassis on eBay that was set up for a roadster, so he sold the first one, and started the process of assembling the chassis himself. The project has taken four and a half years to build so far, and Jim doesn't consider it finished yet. When asked when the car will be finished, his response is, "when I sell it." These projects are never truly finished.

Jim met Ron Mangus in 1988 when Ron did an interior for a '34 Ford Tudor sedan that Jim's son now has. The plan for the roadster interior started early when the body color was chosen. Ron has a good eye for color, and Jim relied on him for material and fabric selection for both the interior and the top. Jim says that while he and Ron selected the colors together, the truth is that Jim really agreed with what Ron thought would look good.

Ron worked with Jim early in the process and constructed a seat and covered it with left over fabric so Jim could get some miles on the car in the "bare metal" stage before it was disassembled for painting. Ron worked closely with Jim to get the seat adjusted just right. The top was another challenge that took a great deal of effort to get it just right as well. Jim is very pleased with the car. It was built to drive and not to show, but the car has been honored with several awards.

Body: All steel by Brookville Roadster, Inc., Brookville, Ohio
Chassis: Roy Brizio Street Rods, San Francisco, California
Paint: "Boyd Yellow" by Tom Rodriguez, Cypress Auto Body, Cypress, California
Engine: Ford 347 small block with three deuces
Drivetrain: Tremec 5-speed transmission, Halibrand quick change rear end
Wheels: Halibrand Sprints, front: 15"×4", rear 15"×10"
Tires: front: Kleiber 145×15", rear: BF Goodrich Silverton 285/70R15

Ron Mangus' Custom Hot Rod Interiors • 25

Jim's '32 has a traditionally styled interior, with plenty of modern lumbar and thigh support designed into the seat. There is a 3-inch strip of carpet on the bottom edge of the doors and kick panel to protect those surfaces from scuffing.

1
The upholstery features light leather piping that highlights the tuck 'n roll seating area and door panels. The contrasting piping is an old school trick that has been around since the '40s and is still effective.

2
The French stitching, pleats, plain smooth leather, and the contrasting piping blend together with a variety of colors and textures creating a more interesting interior.

3
Doors have stock '32 style handles, and the bezels are covered with matching leather.

4
Loop carpet is trimmed with contrasting leather adding visual interest to the floor.

5
The gear shift knob is an old 1932 piece that is made out of onyx. Jim found it during the build process hoping that it might coordinate well with the tan interior. It's a great period piece that goes perfectly in the traditional interior.

1
The '32 has a Bop Top by Sid Chavers. This is a great top, and Ron modified the styling to go better with Jim's car.

2–3
The frame was modified to flatten the top and remove the peak. The minor modifications thinned the top giving it even more of the speedster look he was looking for.

4
The front bow was modified to fit the Steve Moal posts and windshield.

5–6
The trunk repeats the tuck 'n roll pleats and contrasting leather piping.

7
During the build process, Jim and Ron fabricated a compartment under the trunk with room for the battery and essential travel gear. Ron made a removable panel to cover the compartment. There is also enough space between the back of the seat and the removable trunk bulkhead panel to store the top hardware, making the most of the limited space in the car.

8
Sometimes less is more, and in this case, the single stitch line around the leather deck lid liner is all that is needed for a proper finish.

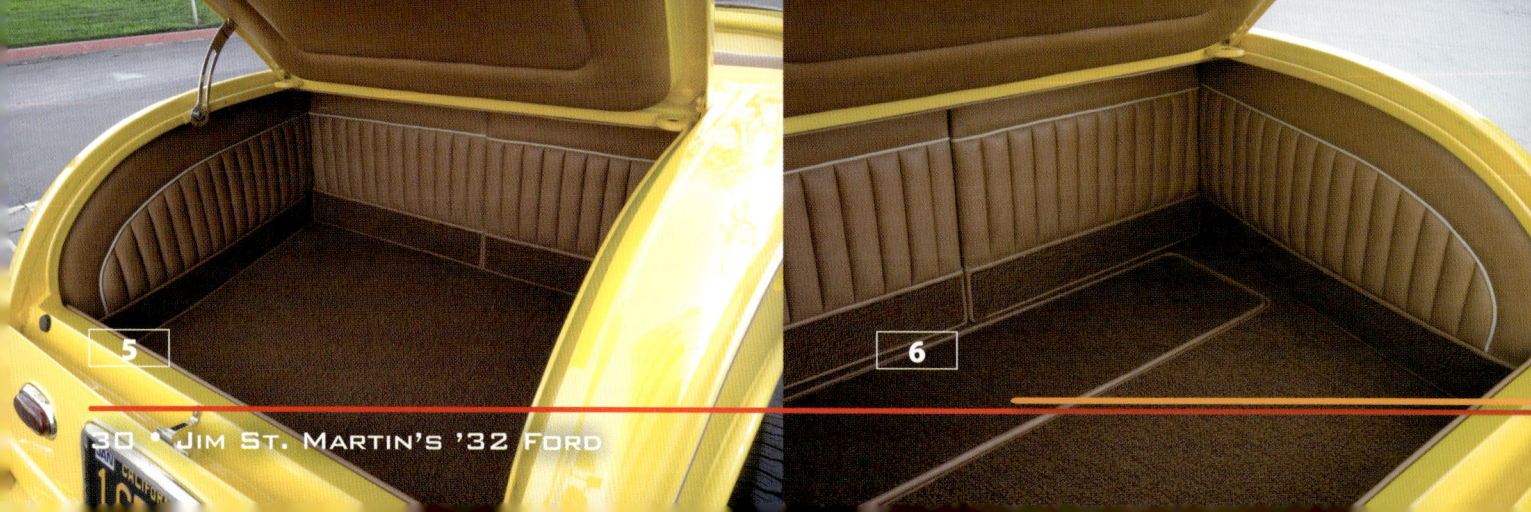

BRUCE McDOWELL'S
'29 Ford

Bruce has quite a drag racing background, competing an alcohol altered dragster, and winning 14 NHRA Wallys in 12 years in the '80s. So it comes as no surprise that he built his own '29 Ford with the help of many good friends. The car was an original Henry Ford '29, was built on '32 rails, and has a '32 grille shell. Bruce stretched the hood and frame 3" to get the engine to fit, assembled the car and had it ready for paint, but then decided to add another 3" right through the middle of the car so he would fit.

He bought the body and frame from a man in San Diego in 1987 who was having a moving sale, so the car was 20 years in the building. Bruce drove it around in primer for six years, afraid that if he took it apart again, it would never get finished. But once he got the process started, it only took him six months to complete, finishing the car on Father's Day 2007.

When it came to the interior, he knew he wanted Ron to do it. As a member of the "Over The Hill Gang," he knew of Ron's reputation through the favorable experiences of other car owners. When he and his wife Debra met with Ron, they were very impressed with Ron's ability to translate their vision into workable ideas. Debra and Ron picked the leathers and colors, and Ron and Ryan designed the interior. To accommodate Bruce's need for room in the car, the seat is as low and set as far back as possible. Bruce describes his experience with Ron as "fabulous."

Body: Original Henry Ford steel body
Paint: Richard Blaisdell, Pine Valley, California
Engine: Chevy 350
Drivetrain: TH350 transmission, Jaguar rear end
Chassis: Highly modified '32 Ford frame rails, pinched, Z'd, with Kugel spindles and components, hand-made stainless A-arms
Wheels: American Racing Torq-Thrust II, front: 16", rear: 18"
Tires: BF Goodrich

This car was a long-term project for Bruce, and Ron feels particularly privileged to have been chosen to do the interior. Ron and his son Ryan designed the interior together. The car was displayed in Ron's booth at the LA Roadster Show, and was invited subsequently by Blackie Gejeian to be shown at the invitation only Fresno Autorama in California.

Leather covered floors help push this interior to a higher level. Custom speaker grilles were shaped to go with the angular design theme. The seat has a substantial thigh bolster with uniquely shaped seat side supports.

1
Bruce is more than six feet tall, so to provide an ample amount of room, Ron made a custom seat frame that sits back and under the rear edge of the body. Notice that the ostrich inlay lines up and runs through the seat back.

2
Custom speaker grilles integrate perfectly into the angular interior theme.

3
Ron and Ryan couldn't come up with a carpet that seemed to work with the interior, so they covered the floor with leather, which pushed the design over the top. They made custom floor mats that are used to protect the leather when the car is driven. Leather is also used to cover the firewall.

4
Ostrich leather inlays add interest and texture to the design.

5
The tightly controlled, angular sculpted shapes that begin with the kick panels run through the doors and into the rear quarter panels, and called for the creation of angular speaker grilles.

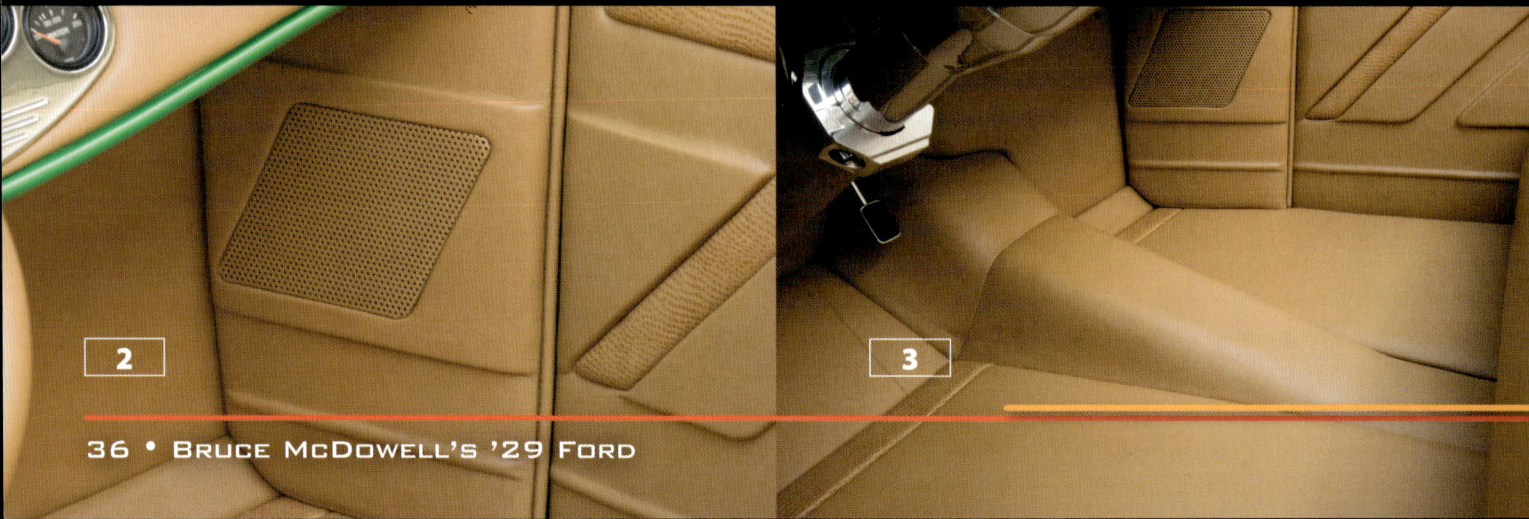

36 • Bruce McDowell's '29 Ford

Ron Mangus' Custom Hot Rod Interiors • 37

1
Notice the steeply angled thigh bolster. Occupants sit low in the car, and the large bolster provides increased support for additional leg room.

2
Ostrich inlays add texture and break up the smooth leather surfaces.

3
The instrument panel didn't escape being leather covered.

4
Ostrich leather was a good choice for the inlay, and the color matches perfectly.

5–6
Trunk has removable floor mat to protect the leather floor.

7
The radio is located above the gas tank, and hidden behind a removable leather covered panel. The sides of the panel are part of the design of the trunk partition, and barely noticeable when the panel is in place.

8
The sculpted design extends from the trunk partition onto the leather covered deck lid liner.

Ron Mangus' Custom Hot Rod Interiors • 39

DANNY SANTORO'S
'32 Ford

Danny had a clear idea of what he wanted in a '32 Ford, but after making a diligent search, just couldn't find what he was looking for. So he decided to build his own, modifying a Wescott body and Frames 'n Thangs frame until he had what he had envisioned. It was unfinished but drivable in 2000. Danny drove the car in black primer, with a borrowed seat from one of Ron's roadsters, to many car shows and Sunday drives, putting 3,000 miles on it in four years. He calls his car " '32 Caliber."

In 2004 Danny began to finish the car working towards entering it in the Grand National Roadster Show in Pomona, California, now that the show had moved from Oakland, California and was so close to home. He devoted every spare moment for the next year and a half to finishing the car.

After having painter troubles, Ron Mangus recommended a shop that was a mere 48-hour round trip to Tomball, Texas. After having a conversation with Randy Borcherding, owner of Painthouse, he knew he had his painter and trailered the car to Texas. Danny had some tense days when a few weeks later Hurricane Rita forced the area to evacuate, but the shop and Danny's car escaped damage.

Danny had worked with Ron Mangus before, and knew he was the one to upholster the car. Ron's creative use of parchment leather and alligator hide make for a one-of-a-kind interior. Other unique features of the interior are the built-in carpeted areas on the floor as an alternative for floor mats, and how the seat backs wrap around into the quarters and doors.

Body: Wescott's Auto, Damascus, Oregon
Body and Paint: Randy Borcherding, Painthouse, Tomball, Texas
Engine: Chevy 350
Drivetrain: 350THM transmission, 9-inch Ford rear end
Chassis: Modified Frames 'N Thangs, Morton, Mississippi
Wheels: Budnik Famosa dished, front: 15"×6", rear: 20"×11"

Ron always had a few seat frames, that only a few people knew about, stashed behind his shop. For several years, Ron had driven his own roadster in primer with a seat from a 1932 five-window coupe. Ron had just finished the roadster, and Danny knew Ron had the seat. "Hey Ron, I need to borrow your seat for three or four months so I can drive my car." Two years later, when Danny was ready for Ron to upholster his roadster, Ron finally got his seat back.

Danny's car is one of Ron's favorite roadsters, probably because he was involved with the car for so many years before it was finished, and because it is so unique. While the car was in primer, Ron helped design the center console that brings the exterior into the interior. This styling change combined with the alligator inlays sets the exotic tone for the entire interior.

Ron Mangus' Custom Hot Rod Interiors • 43

1
Light cream leather with contrasting alligator inserts is wild and exotic. The forms of the seat backs curve outward to the quarter panels, hug the center console, and nest into the body.

2
The floor is trimmed in leather with carpeted inserts. No matter where you look, leather touches leather.

3
A wispy shape with alligator above the armrest brings the leather and alligator theme onto the doors.

4
Danny's concept for the car was that everything be clean and hidden. The ignition switch and other controls are hidden under the instrument panel.

5
The leather instrument close-out panel has perforations instead of speaker grilles, and the front of the interior is finished with a leather firewall cover. The sculpted interior lines of the interior start on the firewall, and are repeated in the trunk.

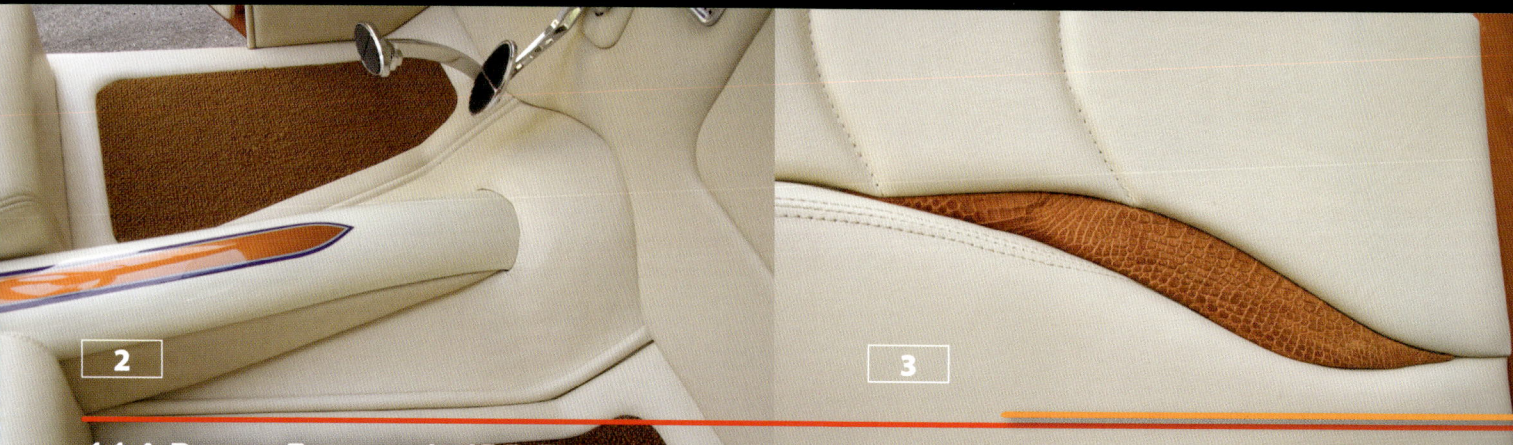

1
Scales from the back of the alligator have a surprising amount of relief and texture. The color of the insert changes slightly from top to bottom to go with the painted copper area on the console.

2–4
Sculpted design starts on firewall, and continues through the kick panel, doors, and onto the rear quarter panels, and ends with the seat back stitching.

5
The armrest shape that begins on the door panel extends onto the quarter panel, making the door panels look visually longer.

6
Electronic shifter control is hidden on the upper part of the firewall, and its location contributes to the clean appearance of the interior.

7
The floor of the trunk received the same styling treatment as the interior floor, with a carpeted insert, so that leather touches leather on all panels.

8
The trunk repeats the interior theme. The deck lid mirrors the design found on the trunk's divider panel.

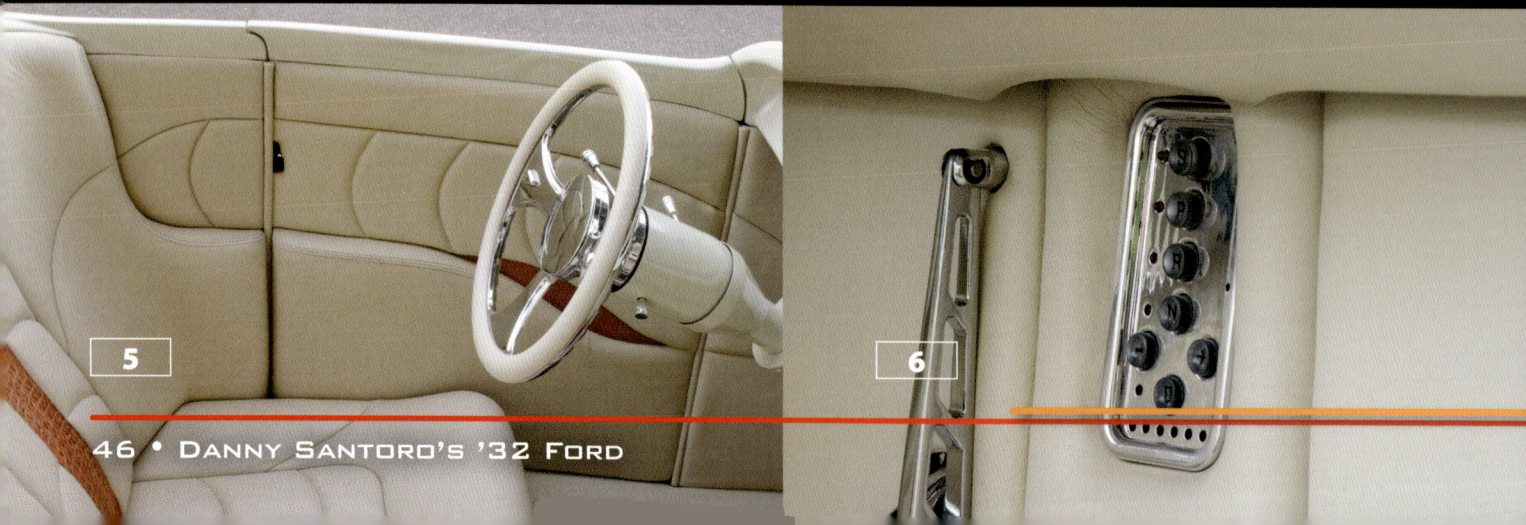

46 • Danny Santoro's '32 Ford

Ron Mangus' Custom Hot Rod Interiors • 47

LEE MARQUEZ'S
'32 Ford

When Linda, Lee's wife, saw the pile of parts in his garage that would eventually become what you see here, she was a bit taken aback at the discovery that the car would have no air conditioning. Now that the car is completed, she enjoys the car as much as Lee does and wouldn't have it any other way.

Lee's '32 Ford was built at home with help from a few friends, including his neighbor Dave, and Ray Becerra who painted the car. It took five years to build, and was completed in January 2007.

Lee bought parts for his '32 from another friend who just happened to live next to Ron's old shop in Bloomington, California, and Lee eventually met Ron. When it was time to do the interior, Lee delivered the car to Ron without fenders or running boards. Some of the interior wiring for the car was not finished, so Lee would go over and work on the wiring at the same time Ron was working on the interior. That afforded several opportunities to modify the seat contours until it was just right, and for them to discuss the design. Lee wanted a simple, traditional tuck 'n roll design, and Ron came through.

One suggestion Ron made was a storage shelf under the dash. Lee was reluctant, but Ron assured him that it wouldn't be noticeable. Once the car was finished, Lee saw the value in that shelf, especially convenient considering the car has no other interior storage.

Body: Harwood Industries, Tyler, Texas
Paint: Ray Becerra
Chassis: Total Cost Involved, Ontario, California
Drivetrain: GM 700R4, Ford 9-inch rear end
Engine: 370 hp Chevy 350, Jon Barrett Hot Rod Engines, Oklahoma City, Oklahoma
Wheels: Intro Retro

Ron cut down the back of the Glide Engineering seat, and sculpted his own foam to provide adequate lumbar and thigh support. Tuck 'n roll pleats are set off by black piping and French stitching.

1
What we have here is an open invitation to enjoy driving a traditional full fendered '32 roadster. The seat back release is on the driver's side of the Glide Engineering lower cushion.

2
Black loop carpet and leather shifter boot bring the exterior color of the car inside, and also are in keeping with the traditional styling of the car.

3
The seat nests under the top edge of the body to maximize legroom, and is closed out by nicely sculptured leather trim that runs around the edge of the body.

4
Vertically pleated tuck 'n roll door panels reinforce the period look. Notice the stealth door pulls that are no wider than the black piping.

5
The instrument panel is clean and simple. Banjo steering wheel picks up the striped effect of the tuck 'n roll pleats. The black leather covered steering wheel also helps convey the traditional feel of the interior.

52 • LEE MARQUEZ'S '32 FORD

Ron Mangus' Custom Hot Rod Interiors • 53

1
The overall presentation of the interior is clean, tight, and traditional, with the look of a tailored pinstriped suit.

2
Budnik banjo steering wheel was the perfect choice, and hints at the old school roots of the interior styling.

3
The vertical tuck 'n roll pleats begin on the kick panels. The angled outline enables the design not to be hidden by the instrument panel.

4
Since this photo was taken, Lee has painted the steering column and support black. Notice the stealth package shelf for loose travel items. It is a very convenient way of adding additional storage to a roadster with limited space.

5–6
Trunk theme repeats the same tuck 'n roll design that is in the interior. There is no bulkhead dividing the trunk from the interior, so the back of the seat is clearly visible. The underside of the deck lid is a leather trimmed fiberglass panel with a simple single sculpted line for interest.

7
The interior trim fits the body shape perfectly.

8
The seat has a nicely formed bolster, and the smooth leather is contrasted by the pleats.

54 • LEE MARQUEZ'S '32 FORD

NATHAN TUTTLE'S
'32 Ford

Nathan is a car enthusiast and antique dealer who knows and appreciates originality. He decided that he wanted the ultimate period correct 1932 Ford hot rod. So he contacted his knowledgeable friend Paul Gommi, winner of eight Dearborn awards, and who has 12 cars in museums including the Ford Museum. Paul knew of an original two-owner '32 owned by a plumber for the past 18 years, and suggested that they look at the car to set a standard for what Nathan was looking for, but with the understanding that the car was not for sale. The '32 was stock and original except for the '48 Ford flathead. It was just what Nathan was looking for. Motivated, Nathan managed to negotiate a deal with the owner too good to pass up, and bought the car.

Nathan wanted to use the stock '32 to build a museum quality hot rod using only NOS parts or old school techniques in any modifications. Paul purchased a 1950 Ford block with overhead valve conversion Ardun heads, built by Don Ferguson who is well known for building and racing these engines. The Ardun OHV conversion was created by the engineer Zora Arkus-Duntov in 1947 to add power to the flathead for heavy-duty use, and became popular with hot rodders once factory OHV V8s became more common for commercial applications.

The car is remarkably well-preserved. The body has never been off of the frame, and was only repainted once by the second owner.

Body: Original Henry Ford '32
Paint: One repaint by the previous owner
Engine: 1950 Ford block with Ardun OHV conversion
Drivetrain: 1939 Ford transmission, 1940 Ford rear end, 1939–48 Columbia 2-speed vacuum overdrive, Halibrand aluminum no-change housing (one of six), circa 1953
Chassis: Original Henry Ford, unmodified. Body never off the frame.
Wheels: 16" 1935 Ford wire wheels with rare 1935 Lyons accessory wheel covers and original '32 stainless-over-steel hub caps
Tires: NOS Firestone, front: 1950 5.00"×16" ribbed racing tires, rear: 1952 7.00"×16"

The interior needed to be re-upholstered, and Paul went to Ron for a stealthy, bomber black leather interior. Ron rebuilt the original seat springs and frame, and preserved the essence of what the car was in its day. Not so readily apparent in the exterior photos are the laid back windshield supports, and the three-inch chop to the top that Paul Gommi did. All of the geometry is worked out so the top still folds down.

This is a traditional old-school '40s style hot rod. Ron rebuilt the original '32 seat, tied down the seat springs, and left the back nice and fat just like it's supposed to be.

1
The seat, doors, kick panels, and rear quarter panels have two-inch pleats like the original.

2
All of the bright trim on the car is original with nickel plating. The 1939 Ford transmission has the stock shifter arm with its wonderful sway to the shape.

3
Paul got these NOS black zinc snaps from Guy Close whose dad bought them from the factory. Ford only made 1,552 Standard roadsters, and Ford would have used these snaps only on those cars. The Deluxe roadsters would have had nickel plated fasteners.

4
The leather pleats line up perfectly with the door panels, quarter panels, and seats.

5
This is the original engine turned instrument cluster originally equipped in this car. A '32 Ford would have only been equipped with amp and gas gauges from the factory. This car is equipped with accessory split gauges installed by the dealer that fit into the same openings. They combined the amp gauge with oil pressure, and the gas gauge with water temperature.

Ron Mangus' Custom Hot Rod Interiors • 61

1
Ron was able to reuse original wood that was on the car to support the top. The snap posts are rare NOS black zinc pieces that would have come on the Standard roadster.

2
The NOS, pre-1960 Stewart Warner gauges are 2-5/8" diameter, with wide bezels and curved glass. They are not reproduced.

3
Additional stitching was added to the original door check straps for detail and strength.

4
Ron repeated the interior pleats in the trunk. Paul Gommi located NOS nickel plated air vents found in classic cars of the era. They allow air to escape from the pressure created when the seat is used.

5
Paul Gommi restored the '39 Ford banjo steering wheel, and the '39 Ford truck steering column drop with the ignition key located at the top. The shifter knob is a custom piece made from inlaid maple.

6
Paul found a '32 hood with blistered sides in the rafters of California Metal Shaping, made by Bill Honda in the '50s. Eric Vaughn louvered the hood and deck lid from a die made in the '50s. Louvers were individually cut out and fit around the hood blisters from a sheet of louvers made in the '50s.

7–8
Headlights and taillights are Electroline from a '40s American LaFrance fire truck.

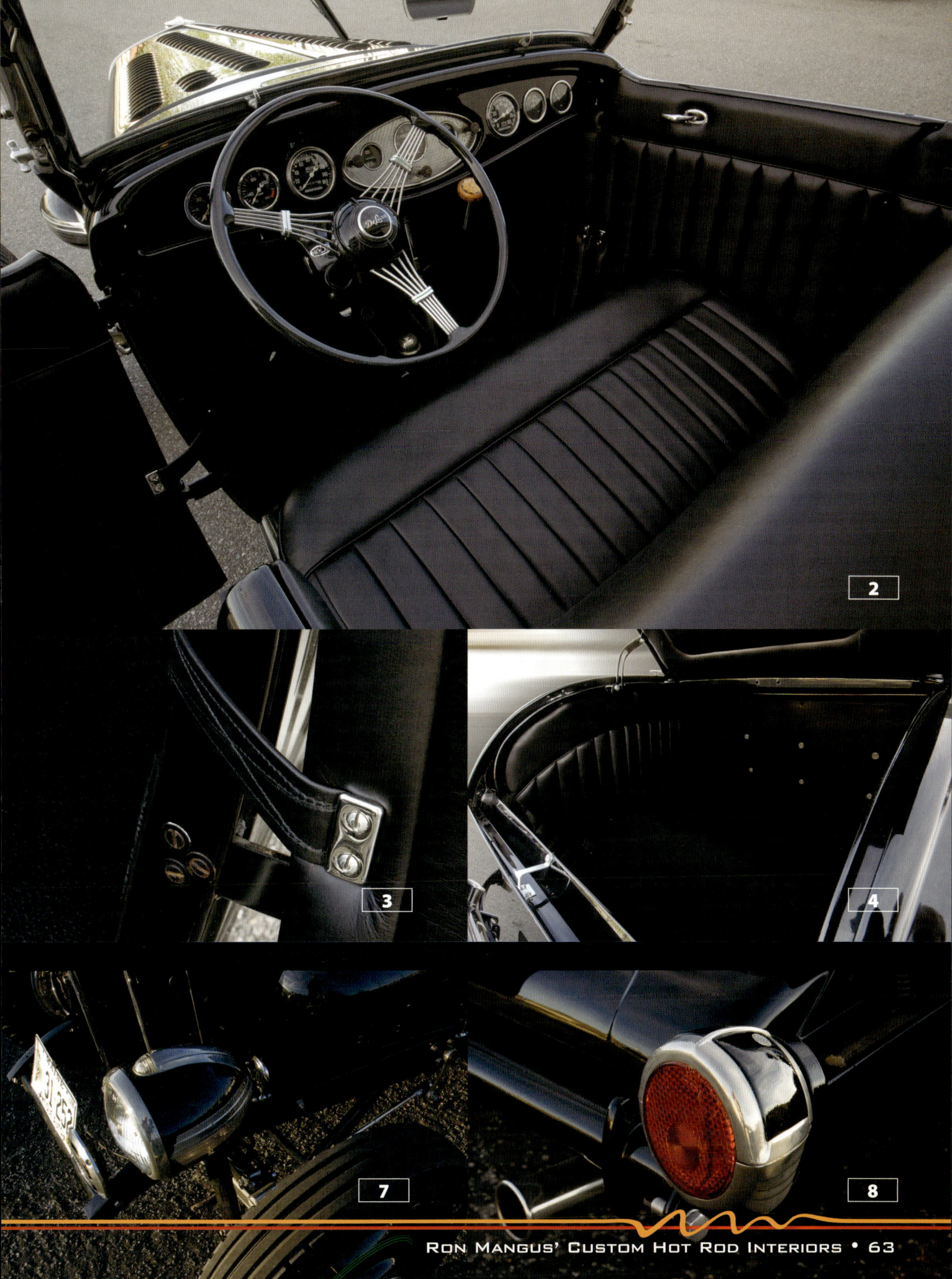

Ron Mangus' Custom Hot Rod Interiors • 63

MATT TACHDJIAN'S
'32 Ford Muroc

The '32 Muroc is the culmination of the efforts of several very talented, well-known names in hot rodding. Jerry Kugel commissioned Chip Foose to design the Muroc, the name being inspired by dry lakes racing in the early days of hot rodding. The car is wider and longer than a stock '32, providing additional interior room and ample space in the engine bay for nearly anything. The hand-made steel car has only lead as filler and only when necessary. Kugel offered ten Hi-boys and ten fendered cars as rolling chassis for customers, and Matt's is roadster number one.

Matt constructed the car in his own shop with the help of a select team of craftsmen. The car has many unique features including custom Hilborn electronic fuel injection. The engine is often mistaken for a big block because of the custom designed billet LS1 coil covers that look like valve covers. Matt also fabricated dual air scoops on the sides of the long hood to add visual interest. The car took two years to build and was finished in December 2005.

After a false start with the first interior, Matt went to Ron for something on the exotic side. Ron suggested frog skin, and it's understandable why frog is used only as accents. Ron designed the sculpted flowing interior lines, and as part of the seat development process, Matt made visits to Ron's shop to have the seat contours fitted for comfort. The sculpted console is hand formed, as are the chrome trim pieces on the doors. The Muroc logo on seat back is billet.

Body: Muroc steel body by Marcel's Custom Metal, Corona, California, designed by Chip Foose, rolling chassis by Kugel Komponents, La Habra, California, number one of ten
Paint: "Bittersweet" by Auto Paint Specialists, Anaheim, California
Engine: Chevy LS1, custom Hilborn electronic fuel injection
Drivetrain: 4L60E, Kugel IRS
Wheels: Billet Specialities Rails, front: 17", rear 20"

The Muroc name brings to mind '40s and '50s dry lakes racing. Ron stylized a cut down, rounded back racing seat and adapted the design for Matt's roadster. The seats are recessed into the back interior panel with a tight gap. The console has an interesting crease that starts at the front of the console, disappears as it gets close the shifter, fades back in at the rear of the control panel door, and then fades out subtly at the top of the rear seat panel.

1
This steering wheel has a split rim so that the top portion can be easily trimmed in leather. Ron covered the back half of the wheel as well. It looks better, and is more comfortable to hold. The seats have a complex, deeply sculptured design with the frog skin inserts.

2
The CNC'ed "Muroc 1" logo draws attention to the fact that this is the first Muroc roadster of ten. The same design is repeated on each of the coil covers on the engine.

3
Ron's supplier of exotic leathers matched the color of the frog skin to the leather sample sent to him.

4
The lower sculpted design line on the doors parallels the seat cushion profile, and also incorporates the same shaped frog skin inlays found on the seat backs.

5
Hand-formed chrome trim tapers to a point, following the body to trim shape. It fits perfectly into a softly sculpted channel.

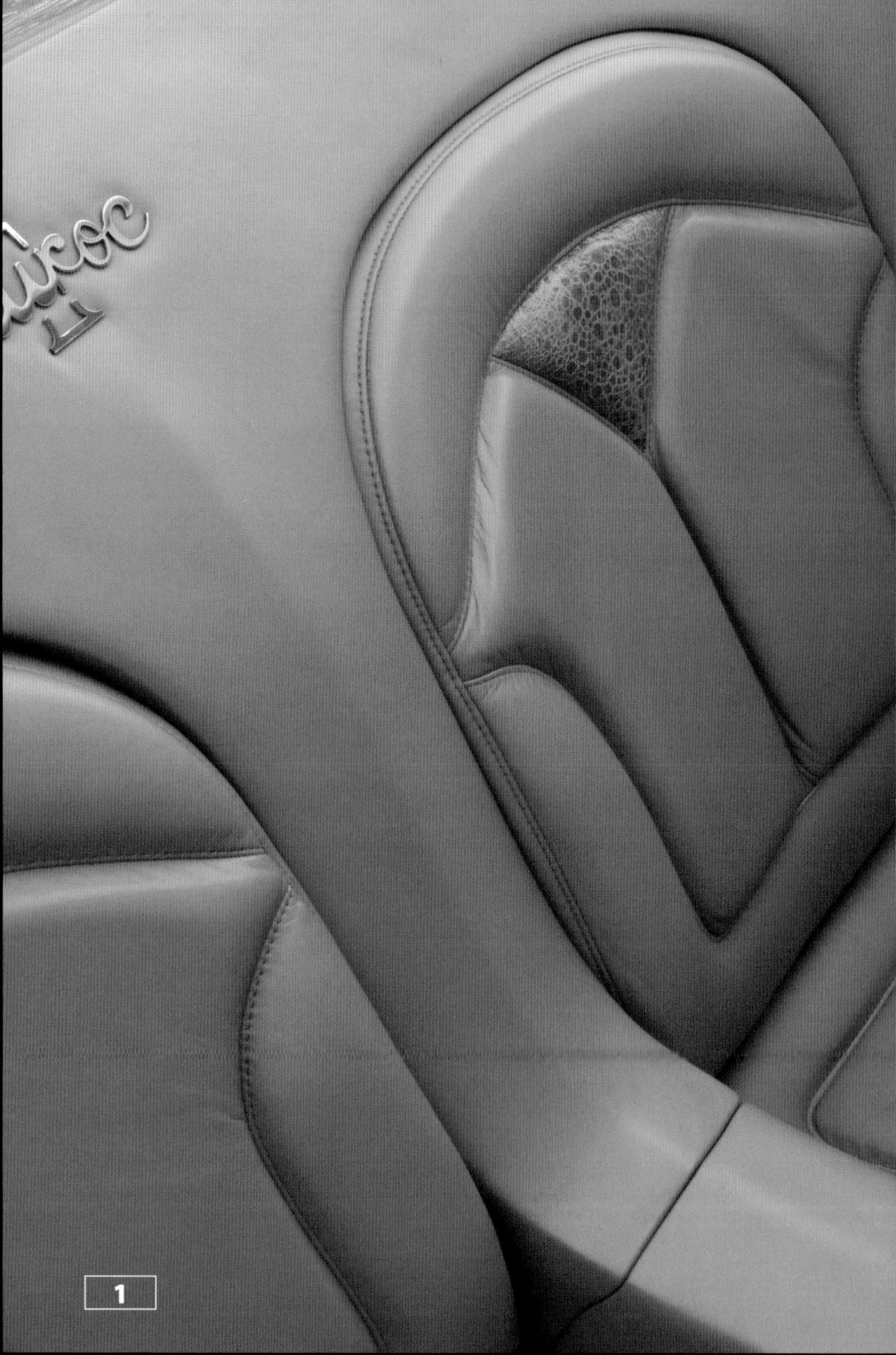

68 • Matt Tachdjian's '32 Ford Muroc

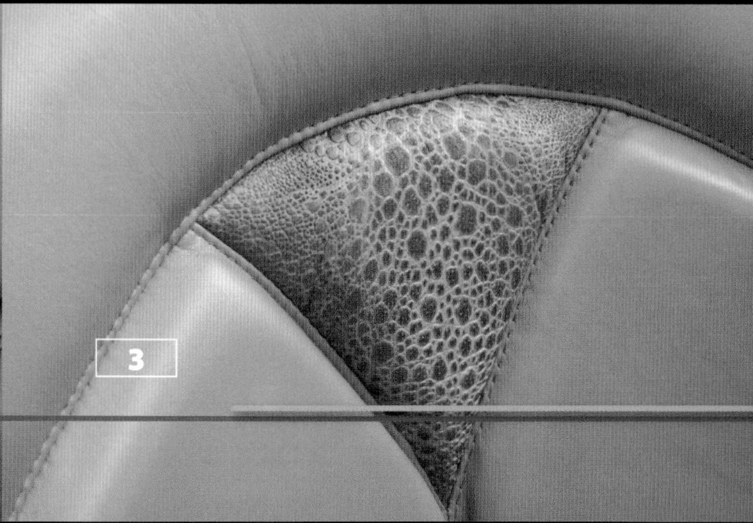

1
Notice the tight fit of the recessed seats into the back panel and the French stitching. The seat, side bolsters and console have very subtle curves and forms. The pattern is deeply sculpted into the foam in this design.

2
The chrome trim begins on the kick panel and carries across the surface of the door panels, ending in an up-swept point, and is recessed into a soft recess in the door.

3
This low view shows off the wild undulating shape of the console, and how the shape relates to the design in the lower door panel and seat cushion profile.

4
The door in the console hides the headlight, ignition switch, and other controls.

5–8
The inside corners of the trunk are curved, which makes for a very custom, fitted appearance. The chrome molding follows the curve and has overlapping joints that help disguise the fact that the center panel is removable. The chrome molding ends in a tapered point for a nice custom touch. A frog skin insert is repeated in the center of the rear panel, and becomes the focal point of the trunk.

Ron Mangus' Custom Hot Rod Interiors • 71

LENN PRITCHARD'S
'32 Ford

Lenn purchased this original, all-steel '32 unpainted and with no interior from Mike Pettit, the rodder who started the project. Mike had stretched the cockpit 3 inches, shortened the deck 3 inches, lengthened the hood 4 inches, widened the car 1 inch, and channeled the car 1½ inches. The rear fenders were bobbed and radiused and molded to the rear roll pan, and the trunk was tubbed. The air exit design on the sides of the hood is repeated on the third brake light and the taillights. One of the more striking details is the one piece windshield and the way the posts disappear into the cowl. There's much more, but there is not room here to tell the whole story.

The ZR1 engine is all dressed up in polished aluminum and chrome. When first installed it would not run properly, and it took six months to diagnose the ZR1's aftermarket computer system. But "ITLFLY" is now all sorted out and runs great.

Lenn and Ron worked closely together on the interior design. Ron created the custom bench seat, and covered it with Connolly leather. Other interior features include GPS and stereo controls that are displayed on an LCD screen that pops out from a hidden panel in the front of the console.

The stretched interior combined with the power and handling translates into comfort with an attitude.

Body: Original all-steel '32 Ford. Body work by Mike Pettit, Dent, Michigan
Paint: PPG Real Red by Randy Lavin, Watertown, Pennsylvania
Engine: Chevy ZR1 crate motor
Drivetrain: 700R4 transmission, Kugel 9-inch rear end
Chassis: Kugel front and rear suspension
Wheels: Budnik, front: 15"×7", rear: 17"×10"
Tires: Nitto

Ron Mangus' Custom Hot Rod Interiors • 73

Ron fabricated this interior in 1998, so it shows some of the techniques and styling that were popular at that time. For example, cloth material was used to hide the speakers in the rear quarter panels. Because of the three-inch stretch in the interior, the seats are so far back in the car that armrests were placed in the quarter panels.

1
Ron fabricated the seat and frame for the car, and also molded the seat divider and back trim piece from fiberglass. The lower edge of the back trim becomes a design line that continues through the rear quarter panels and onto the doors, where it changes directions and loops back toward the rear on the lower part of the door. The other sculpted shapes in the door panel are repeated in the seating areas providing continuity to the entire design theme.

2
Highly styled console supports the GPS and stereo system. The carpet detail on the side of the console is repeated on the kick panels.

3
Notice the leather wrapped shifter knob and matching leather boot. The shape of the console cover is carefully designed to go with the theme of the interior.

4
Parking brake boot is covered in matching leather.

5
The sculpted, highly styled armrest was carved from foam, then wrapped in leather.

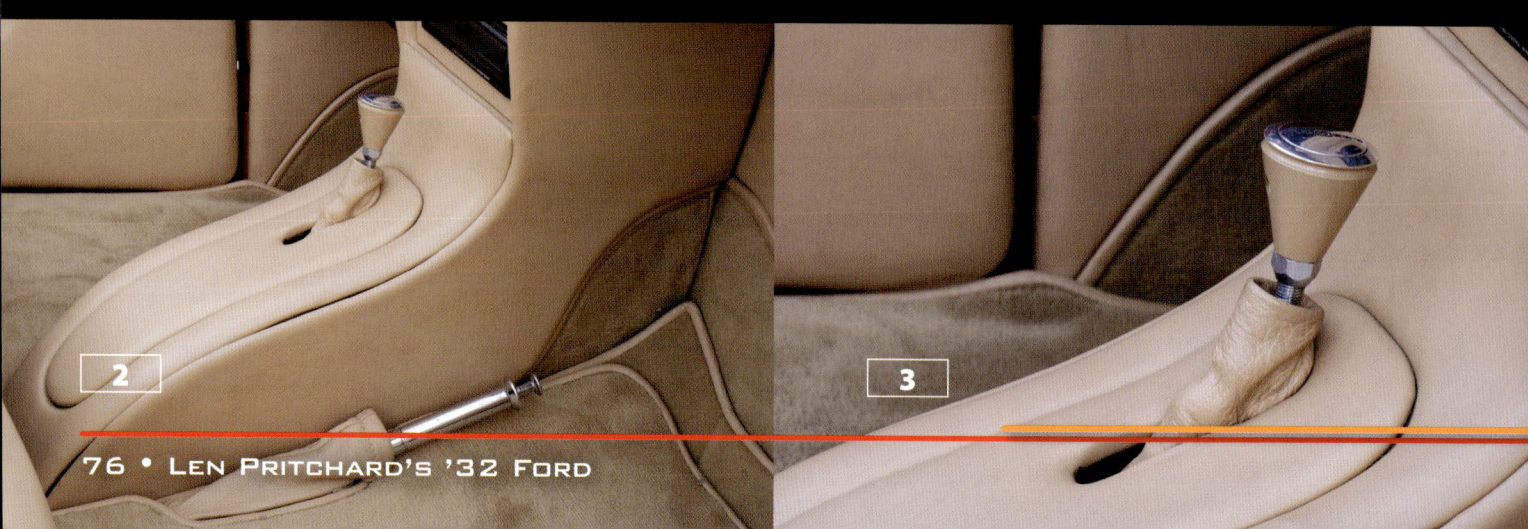

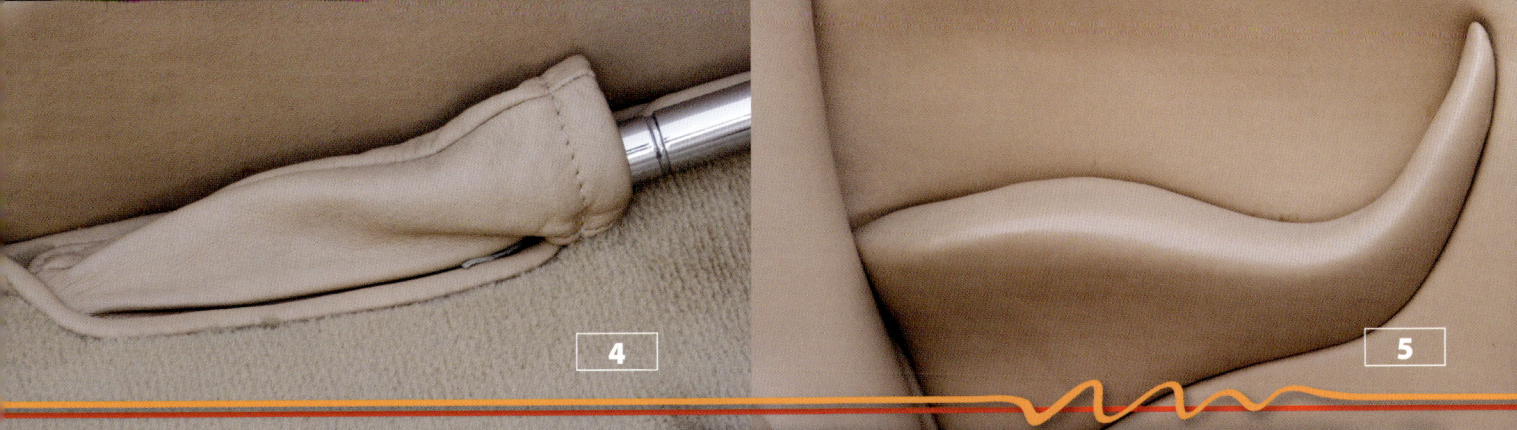

Ron Mangus' Custom Hot Rod Interiors • 77

1
Lenn's '32 has a serious 400 watt sound system, and the rear speakers are hidden behind cloth grilles. There is a softly sculpted scoop to provide a recess for the armrest.

2
The instrument panel is from a '32 sedan, and the red paint certainly brings the exterior color into the interior.

3
The kick panels were sculpted and made from fiberglass to house the uniquely shaped, cloth covered speaker grilles.

4
The carpeted area on the kick panel not only adds visual interest, but also helps to protect the light leather from scuffs. There are curved extensions on the side edges of the console for a bit of extra styling.

5–6
The inside corners of the trunk close-out panels are curved, giving it a "fitted luggage" look. The carpeted strip on the panels adds interest and helps protect the leather.

7
There is a raised design on the leather covered deck lid panel.

8
The oval instrument cluster really looks great in the car.

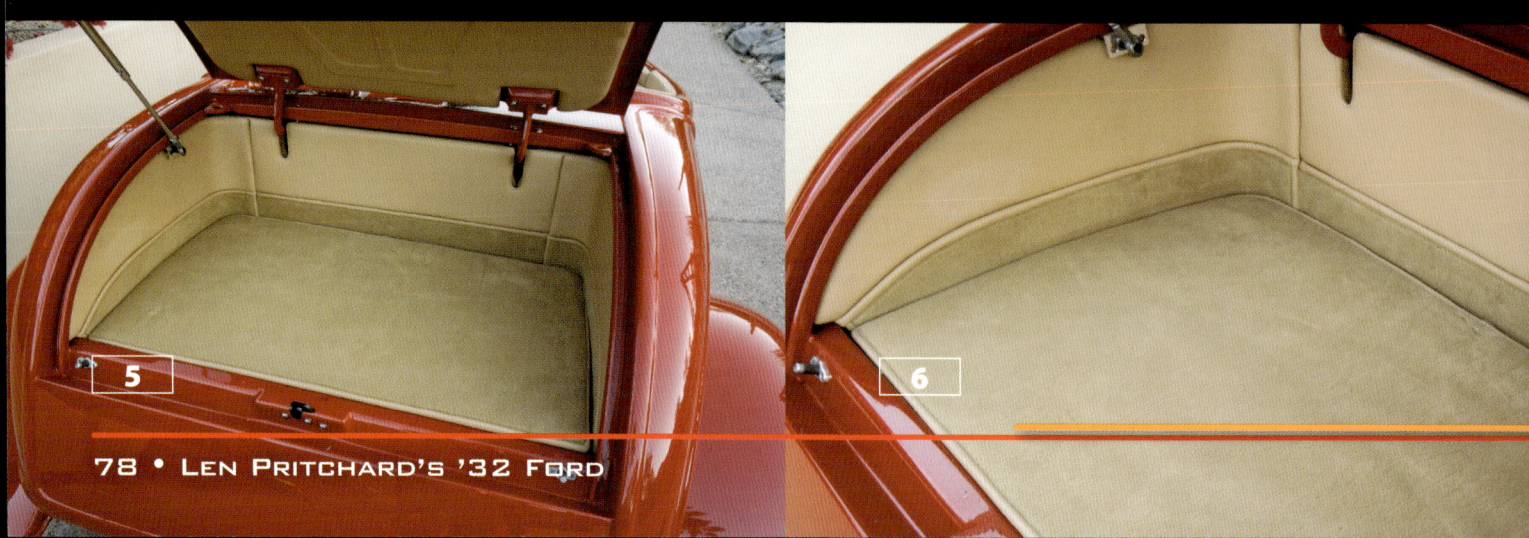

MARV ANDERS'
'34 Ford

Marv always wanted a 1934 Ford roadster, so when he was finally able to actually get serious, he started a diligent search for a car. He found this car online in Florida, but needed to see and touch the car before making his decision. After flying back home to California, he bought the car, and had it shipped to California in July 2004. Marv is really pleased with the car. "It runs, rides, and drives great."

The Gibbon body is painted Porsche red, and Bob White of California Customs and Classics in Fontana, California, did modifications to the body, brakes, frame, and installed a new polished aluminum grill.

Marv went to Ron to re-upholster the interior, not really knowing what he wanted. Ron created a very tasteful and tailored interior that greatly enhanced the overall curb appeal of the car. The design theme Ron created is consistently carried through from the dash to the trunk. "Hard-look" sculpted tan leather is used throughout the interior. Red leather accents add rich detail, and the red stitching adds a finishing touch. Ron also upholstered the Carson-style top.

In talking to Marv, you can tell he really likes his '34. He's won many awards with the car, two being best of show.

Body: Gibbon, Ringgold, Virginia, with steel hood and side panels
Paint: Porsche red, original painter unknown
Engine: 351 Ford Cleveland
Drivetrain: C6 transmission, Ford 9-inch rear end
Chassis: Reproduction '34 Ford with Heidt Mustang II front suspension
Wheels: 15" American Racing Torq-Thrust II
Tires: BF Goodrich

Ron Mangus' Custom Hot Rod Interiors • 81

Ron completely reworked the Glide Engineering seat, covering it with reshaped foam. The wavy seat insert design is repeated on the door panels, and the horizontal sculpted lines are found on the doors and leather covered instrument panel. Red accents on the seats and armrest bring some of the exterior red into the car.

1
The reworked Glide Engineering seat fits perfectly in the car. The way the front of the seat is trimmed where the stitching and leather runs from the seat cushion to the floor, interrupting the side bolster, is called a waterfall design. Red accent stitching is used throughout the interior.

2
The shifter and brake lever have leather boots.

3
The instrument panel is leather covered, and the design features three sculpted speed lines on each side of the instrument cluster, matching the upper part of the door panels. The stereo is mounted underneath in a leather-covered housing.

4
Three sculpted speed lines and the red leather armrest add interest to the upper section of the door panels.

5
There is a very tight fit with no gaps between the door and kick panels. The door release is positioned low on the doors.

84 • Marv Anders' '34 Ford

Ron Mangus' Custom Hot Rod Interiors • 85

1
The depth in the seat pattern is accomplished by using a high density foam. The shapes are cut out, and glued to the underlying foam, covered in leather, and finished by stitching on each side of the grove.

2
The Glide Engineering seat back tilts forward, providing access to behind the seat storage. There is plenty of room for two 6"×9" speakers, and a covered storage compartment trimmed in matching leather.

3
The rear compartment trim wraps around and overlaps the rear quarter panels. The seats are nicely shaped with full, flowing forms.

4
The deck lid was removed and the hinges painted to match the leather. This is a small detail, but the red hinges were too pronounced against the tan leather.

5–6
The power deck lid features a linear actuated motor that moves the support rod back and forth to raise or lower the deck lid. The leather-covered housing is mirrored on both sides for symmetry. The design on the seats is repeated on the back panel.

7
Custom paint detail is a nice touch on the car's rear quarter panels.

Ron Mangus' Custom Hot Rod Interiors • 87

SO-CAL'S
'32 Ford

You've no doubt seen SO-CAL's 1932 Ford in magazines, and perhaps in person. It's a rolling billboard, advertising SO-CAL's line of hot rod products. What you might not have realized is that Ron Mangus did the interior. This car was completed by SO-CAL in September 1999.

The SO-CAL '32 Hi-boy started a revolution in hot rodding in the '90s. They offered complete turnkey cars, or a customer could purchase all the parts necessary to build his own. It was a real trendsetter, bringing back the nostalgia of old school hot rodding. This car features the time-tested trademark logo and red and white paint scheme SO-CAL's founder Alex Xydias used for all of his hot rods, race cars, and tow vehicles in the early '50s, including the famous Belly Tank racer that ran 198 mph at Bonneville in 1952.

Ron's traditional brown tuck 'n roll leather interior is perfect for the car, adding the authentic touch that no doubt contributed to the car's commercial success. The seat is comfortable and offers ample padding and lumbar support uncharacteristic of the '50s when little attention was paid to creature comfort. The interior has held up incredibly well for so many years considering the use the car gets as a demonstrator and vendor display car.

Body: All steel by Brookville Roadster, Inc., Brookville, Ohio
Paint: SO-CAL Speed Shop, Pomona, California
Engine: Chevy ZZ 430 Chevy
Drivetrain: 700R4, Ford 9-inch rear end
Chassis: SO-CAL Speed Shop, Pomona, California
Wheels: 16" SO-CAL knock-off Hot Rod
Tires: Firestone, front: 5.50"×16"; rear: 7.50"×16"

Ron Mangus' Custom Hot Rod Interiors • 89

When Pete Chapouris started to build these SO-CAL roadsters, he called on Ron to design an interior that went back to the roots of the '32. Ron proposed chocolate brown leather with matching German square-weave carpet to keep it simple and nostalgic.

1
Ron's design looks great and has several practical and functional features. The carpet on the lower edge of the door and kick panel are nice design elements and also protect the lower surfaces against scuffing.

2
SO-CAL's banjo steering wheel is at home in this roadster. The straight spokes go great with the straight three inch tuck 'n roll pleats.

3
On the steering column support a Southern California Timing Association medallion reminds us of the rodding world of the late '40s.

4
Straight forward pleated door panel design has a smooth leather upper and carpeted lower edge.

5
Kick panel pockets, pleated to match the door, provide needed interior storage for loose items.

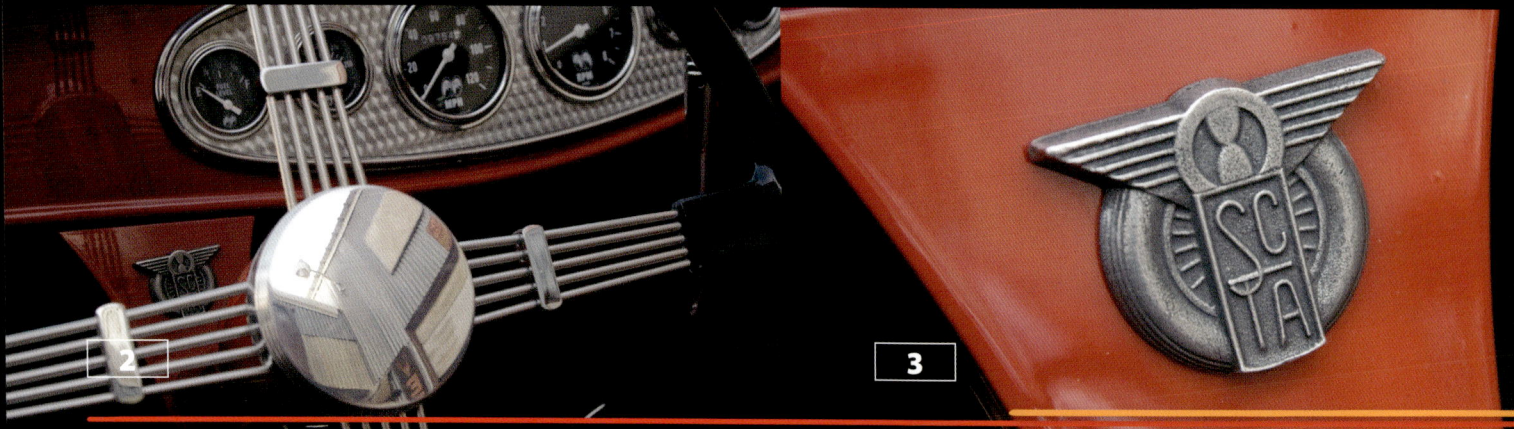

92 • SO-CAL'S '32 FORD

Ron Mangus' Custom Hot Rod Interiors • 93

1
The trimmed down Glide Engineering seat reclines, slides forward and backward, and the seat back is low enough to slide underneath the edge of the body providing additional legroom.

2
The simple instrument panel with its oval engine turned cluster, banjo steering wheel, and tall shifter are all the right things that belong in a traditional '32.

3
The interior door handle is a '32 design with a chrome bezel.

4
The piping starts on the kick panels, runs through the doors, onto the rear quarter panels, and lines up with the piping on the seat back.

5
Located to the right of the gas pedal, just like in the '30s, is a small round actuator on the floor for setting the cruise control. It was a mechanical device then.

6
Both shifter and brake release leather boots are double French stitched.

7
Door check straps have the SO-CAL logo.

8
German square-weave carpet is installed without close-out panels to make use all of the available trunk space.

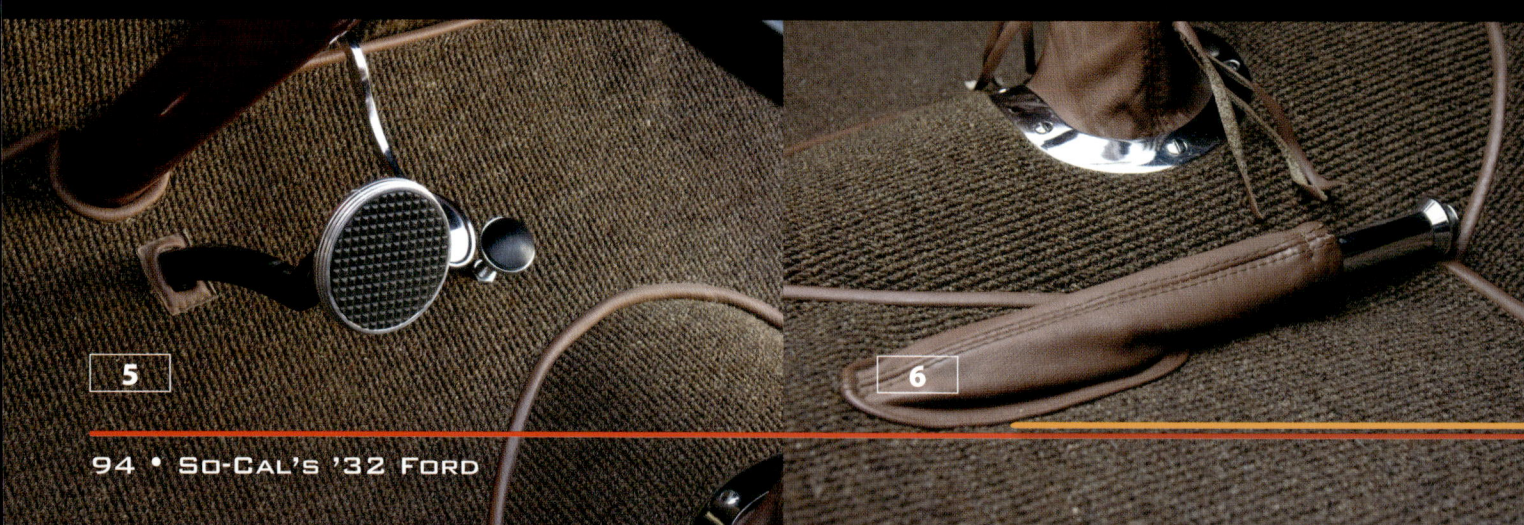

GEORGE JOHNSON'S
'32 Ford

George longed for another open car ever since he sold his '59 fuel-injected Corvette, and decided that a '32 roadster was what he wanted to build to replace it. He found this incomplete roadster as a rolling chassis with no drivetrain. George then found an engine from a late model Camaro SS from a wrecking yard with only 6,000 miles on it.

Fred's Custom Wiring in Ontario, California, built the car. George has known Fred since the '80s, when Fred did the wiring for a '34 Ford pickup that George had at the time. George has a lot of respect for Fred and his team and the great deal of pride they have in their work.

When it came time for paint, Fred mixed samples until he found what George was looking for, a deep grape with a bit of pearl. The car took a year and a half to build, and was completed in 2000.

Ron worked with George to come up with an interior design that had the right blend of traditional hot rod and show car. Ron designed wildly sculpted, organic door panels with contrasting pleated inserts.

George's bugs-in-the-teeth roadster has brought a great deal of enjoyment and many fond memories to his family while cruising the streets of Upland, California, and it has been worth all of the time, work and money it took to get there.

Body: Hannemann Fiberglass, Azusa, California
Paint: Pearl Grape, Fred's Custom Wiring, Ontario, California
Engine: Chevy LT1 350
Drivetrain: TH350, Ford 9-inch rear end
Chassis: Total Cost Involved, Ontario, California
Tires: BF Goodrich
Wheels: 15" Halibrand Sprints

Ron Mangus' Custom Hot Rod Interiors • 97

The interior is trimmed in light lilac and purple leathers. The seat is full and plush, with pleated leather inserts and French stitching. Door panels are deeply sculpted.

1
Ron's design is wild and unrestrained. The seat is plush and comfortable with a luxury car feel.

2
Rear speaker grille is surrounded by a uniquely shaped purple leather panel.

3
A padded glove compartment is in the lower instrument panel cover that also hides air conditioning plumbing.

4
Kick panel has a lower carpeted area that visually helps to lower the floor and also protects the panel.

5
The organic raised speaker shape necks down and continues onto the door panel, and the grille has been painted to match.

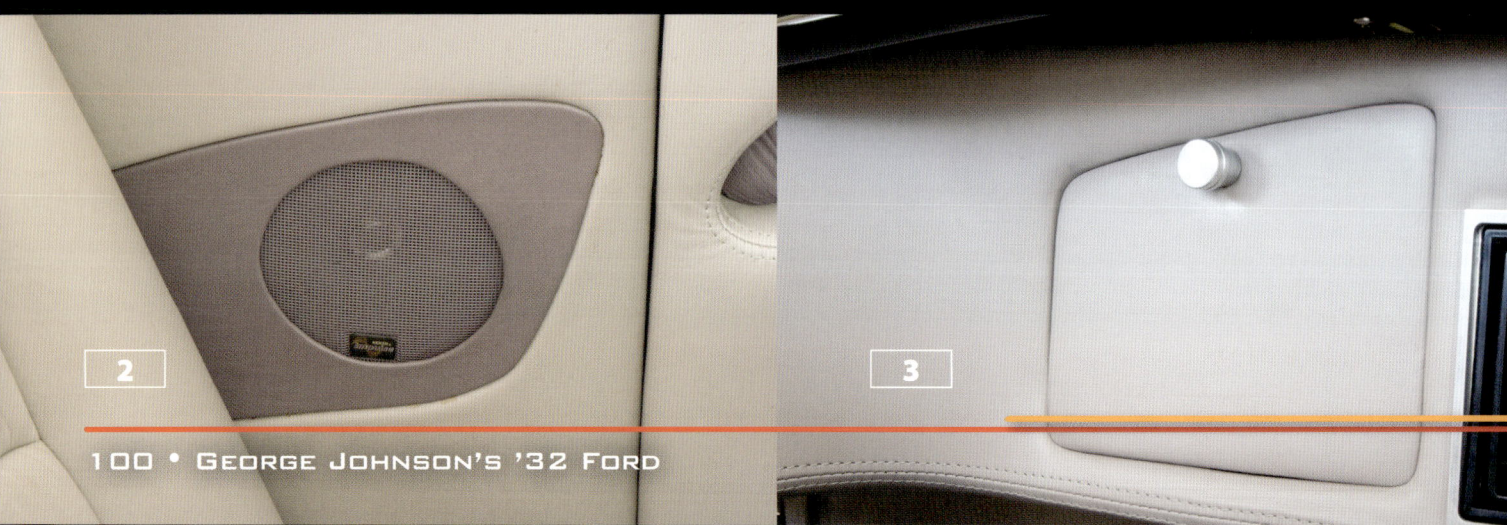

Ron Mangus' Custom Hot Rod Interiors • 101

1
The door panels have windswept shapes that are deeply embossed into the surface.

2
The lower armrest blends smoothly out of the door panel, while an opening in the surface of the upper door panel is finished in pleated, purple leather providing functional clearance.

3–4
The lower instrument panel cover is smoothly shaped and houses the sound system controls, glove compartment, and air conditioning vents. Tweeters were placed in the upper part of the kick panels.

5
The armrest opening is nicely shaped and detailed.

6–8
The trunk is finished in the same leathers as the interior. The underside of the deck lid has sculpted design lines, and the trunk release mechanism is concealed in a leather-covered box.

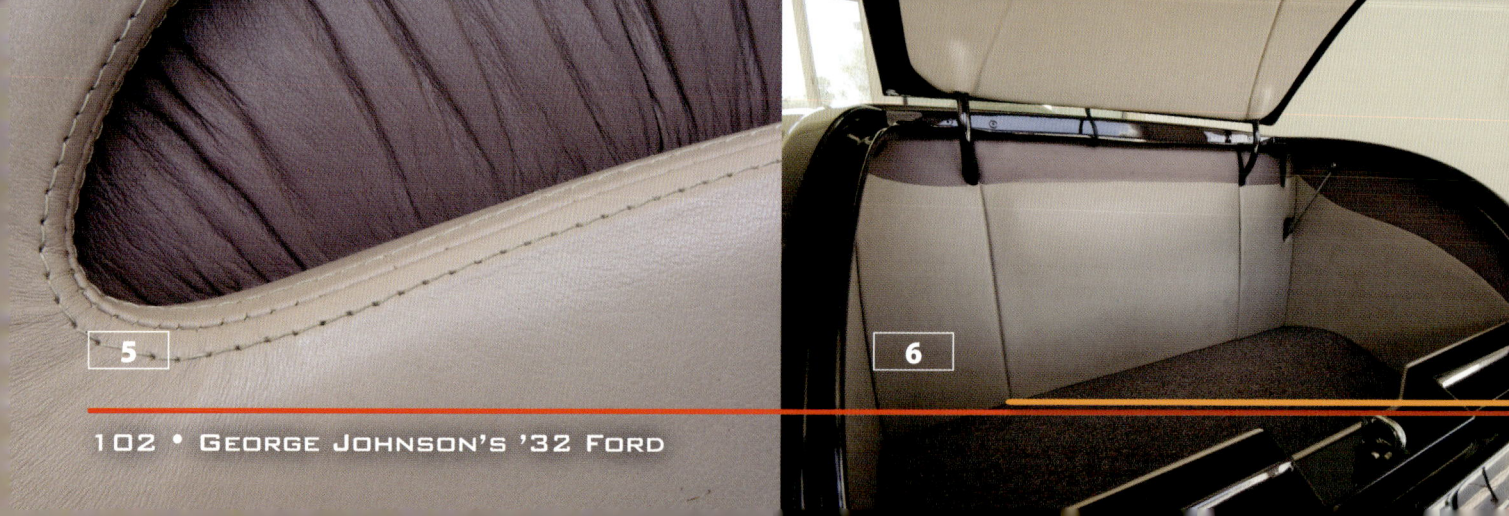

RICHARD SEALS'
'35 Ford

Richard's roadster was literally a barn find. The conversion to a hot rod had been started in the '60s, but the project was abandoned, and the car left in pieces. Richard's transformation of the car is masterfully executed, and the car was finished in December 2007.

In the process of restoration, Richard discovered that the deck lid hinges could be reversed, so that the trunk could be converted into a rumble seat. However, if the car was to have a rumble seat, there had to be an interior panel designed to provide space for the floor of the rear compartment. This gave Ron the opportunity to create a unique fiberglass cover that became the focal point of the interior.

Ron first met Richard at the LA Roadster show. Richard brought a massive smile and a check to secure a slot in Ron's schedule.

Ron's interior is stunning. Inspired by the thin chrome moldings on the sides of the hood, he created the large cover behind the seats and made a waterfall design using custom fabricated inlaid chrome moldings. The bright trim repeats in the doors, and also relates to the spokes of the banjo steering wheel.

The cover's recessed seats and sculpted form lead the eye towards the deck lid, and the same form then sweeps downward to the rear of the car. The sculpted lines of the console, armrest, and door panels blend together perfectly.

Body: Original steel 1935 Ford
Paint: Candy Brandywine by Retro Auto Works, Harbor City, California
Engine: Corvette 350
Drivetrain: TH400, Ford 9-inch rear end
Chassis: Modified stock
Wheels: 17" American Racing Ansen® Sprint
Tires: Pirelli

Ron Mangus' Custom Hot Rod Interiors • 105

The interior was not designed with a cover like this originally. After a lot of consideration and planning, Ron created a cover made from fiberglass, and designed pockets to recess the Mercedes seats. The seats were three inches higher than the doors, so they were cut down to fit into the car, reshaped and recontoured.

1
Console flows forward from instrument panel, then reverses direction and heads to the back. Recesses are sculpted on the sides of the console to provide additional floor clearance. Custom inlaid chrome trim is recessed into sculpted recesses in the door panels.

2–3
The seat and sound system controls are hidden underneath the center armrest. The Mercedes seats were tough to work with. The seat controls had to be removed from the sides of the seats because of the lack of room. The seats were rewired and the controls moved to the console.

4
The armrest, with its windswept, tapered form, is an interesting sculpture in its own right. All of the chrome moldings were custom fabricated.

5
The shapes of the seats, console, door panels, and armrest use the same vocabulary of forms and blend together beautifully.

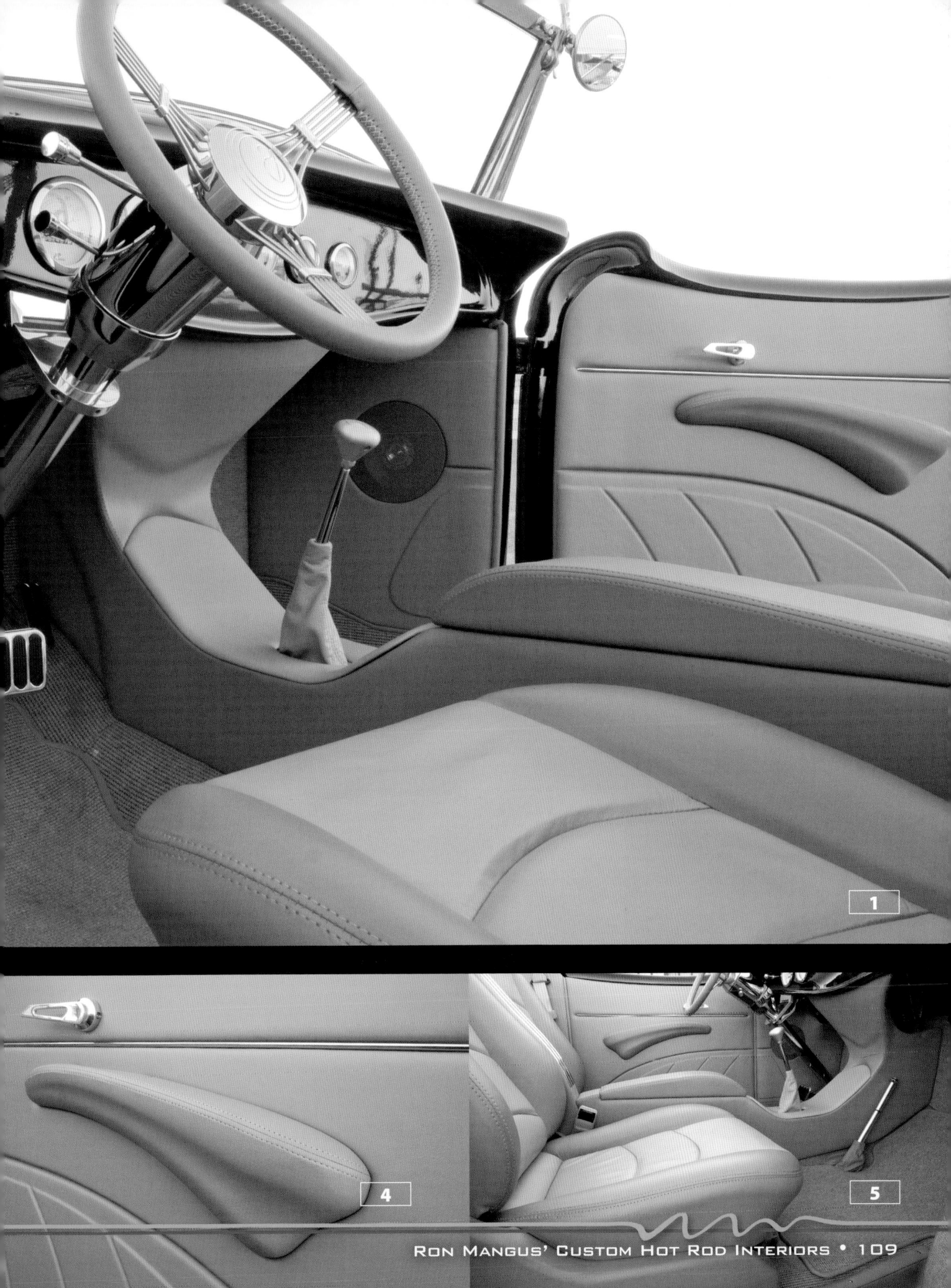

1
Three chrome moldings waterfall down the rear fiberglass shell following the shape created by the seat's side bolsters.

2
The rumble seat compartment is finished to match the interior. Ron designed a leather molding that fits tightly to the opening to finish the edge.

3
Ron used the shapes found on the instrument panel and the interior to sculpt the panels inside the rumble seat.

4
The leather-covered box encloses the battery.

5
Ron designed his interior to go with the '35 roadster's sweeping forms.

6
The lower carpeted area on the door panels tapers out on the kick panels. The flooring and mats are made from German square-weave carpet.

7
Door panel design ends in a smoothly shaped kick panel.

8
The seat design is echoed on the rumble seat.

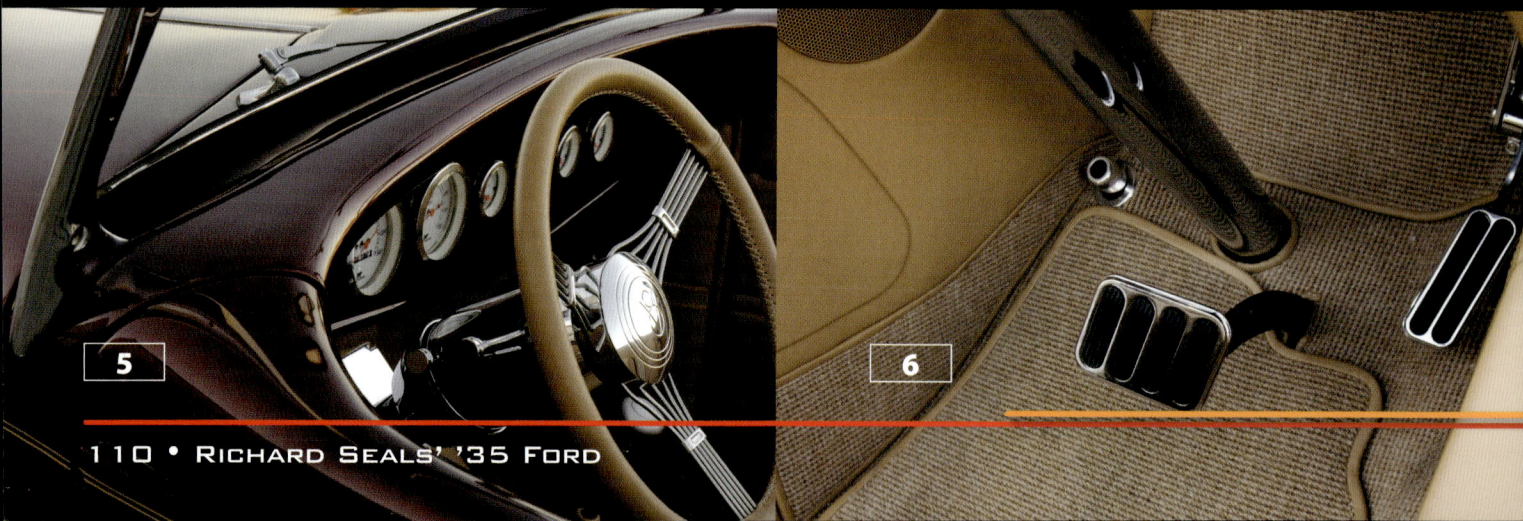

BOB GORY'S
'33 Ford

Bob always wanted a '33 Ford. He finally found and purchased the body, hood, and a few other pieces in Phoenix from the owner who started the project but lost interest. Bob and his son Dino roughed the car together using a TCI chassis, then took the car to Tommy's Auto Fabrication in Riverside, California for more assembly and the installation of the drivetrain.

The car first had an airbag suspension, but Bob didn't like the way it felt, so they reworked the suspension using coil-overs. STS Customs in Upland, California did the final assembly and paint. Figuring out what color to paint the car wasn't an issue, as all of Bob's hot rods have always been red. In fact, all of his other cars are red as well.

Bob had known Ron for several years, and after a short conversation about the general direction of the car's interior design, Ron seemed to know exactly what Bob as looking for, and came up with many good ideas that Bob appreciated. One challenge was to come up with the right red leather that went with the exterior, and Ron came up with the perfect match. Bob said that he had a great experience working with Ron, and the results speak for themselves.

Body: Wescott's Auto, Damascus, Oregon
Paint: STS Kustoms, Upland, California
Engine: Chevy 350, dual quads
Drivetrain: 700R4 transmission, Currie aluminum rear end
Chassis: Total Cost Involved, Ontario, California
Wiring and sound: Pomona Valley Customs, Ontario, California
Wheels: Colorado Custom Wheels, Winter Park,
　　　front: 16"×7", rear: 18"×8"
Tires: Toyo, front: 195/50R16, rear: 225/65R18

Ron has customers that Bob knows, so Bob was accustomed to Ron's style and quality. Bob wanted a gray interior at first, but Ron suggested red on red, and found a red leather that matched the paint color perfectly, bypassing the process of having leather custom dyed. Bob lives in Arizona, so he and Ron communicated via phone and Internet to discuss the design and review progress.

1
Everything in the interior is either chrome or red, with black details. Speed lines are sculpted into the door panels, and taper back to normal surface, ending on an angle. Armrest shape grows out of the door panel.

2
The armrest form resolves at the end of the door, but the upper design line continues onto the quarter panel.

3
The top of the console is split for mechanical access, and the cover is nicely shaped and becomes part of the design.

4
Sound system and air conditioning controls are located in the forward part of the console. The black control face and vent serve as accents to the all-red interior.

5
The flooring and carpet is German square-weave carpet. The hand brake is finished with a chrome bezel and a red leather boot.

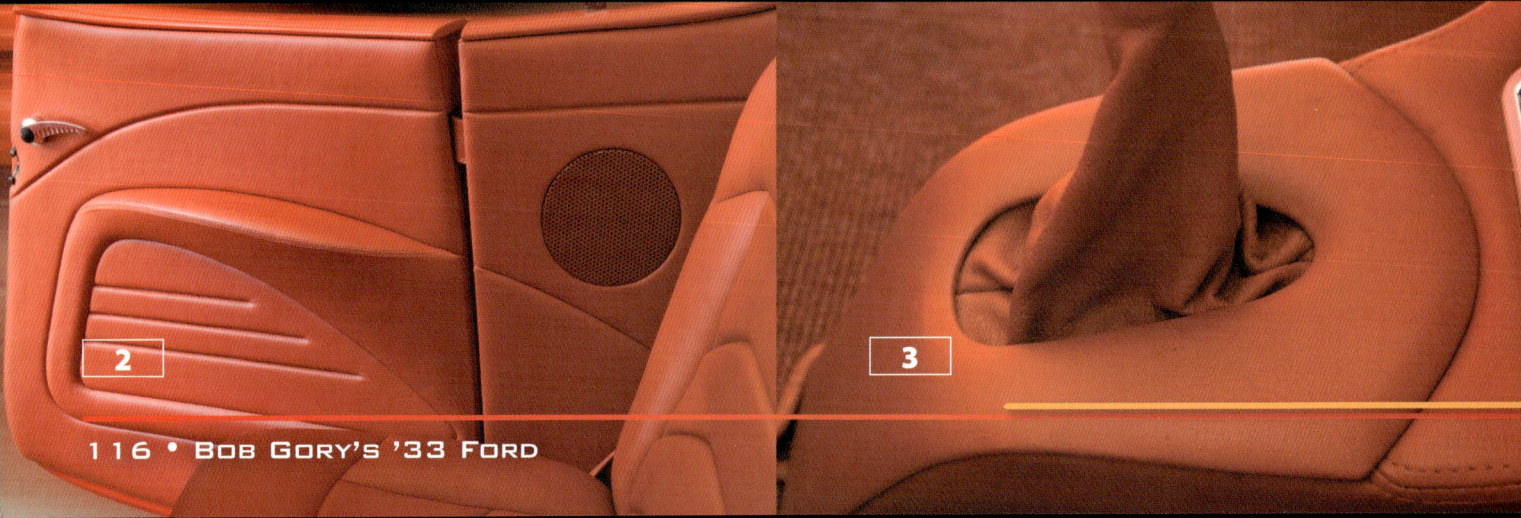

116 • Bob Gory's '33 Ford

Ron Mangus' Custom Hot Rod Interiors • 117

1
The Glide Engineering seat folds forward allowing for storage behind the seat. The pleated leather storage pocket runs the full width of the interior providing a place to stash loose items.

2
The interior design consists of a pleasing array of shapes and forms, with interesting resolutions of lines and good placement of graphic elements that add focal points to the design.

3
The design of the seat cushion is mirrored in the seat back.

4
The small console is well integrated into the design.

5
The car has a 400 watt sound system. Painted speaker grilles are placed in the kick panels and quarter panels.

6–8
Bob is going to use this car. A four-inch strip of carpet on the front and sides of the trunk helps protect the leather areas against scuffing from things placed in the trunk. The decklid repeats the sculpted design from the interior. The tapered speed line design seen on the door panels is repeated in the trunk surrounded by a sculpted outline. An opening in the left panel accommodates the power deck lid mechanism.

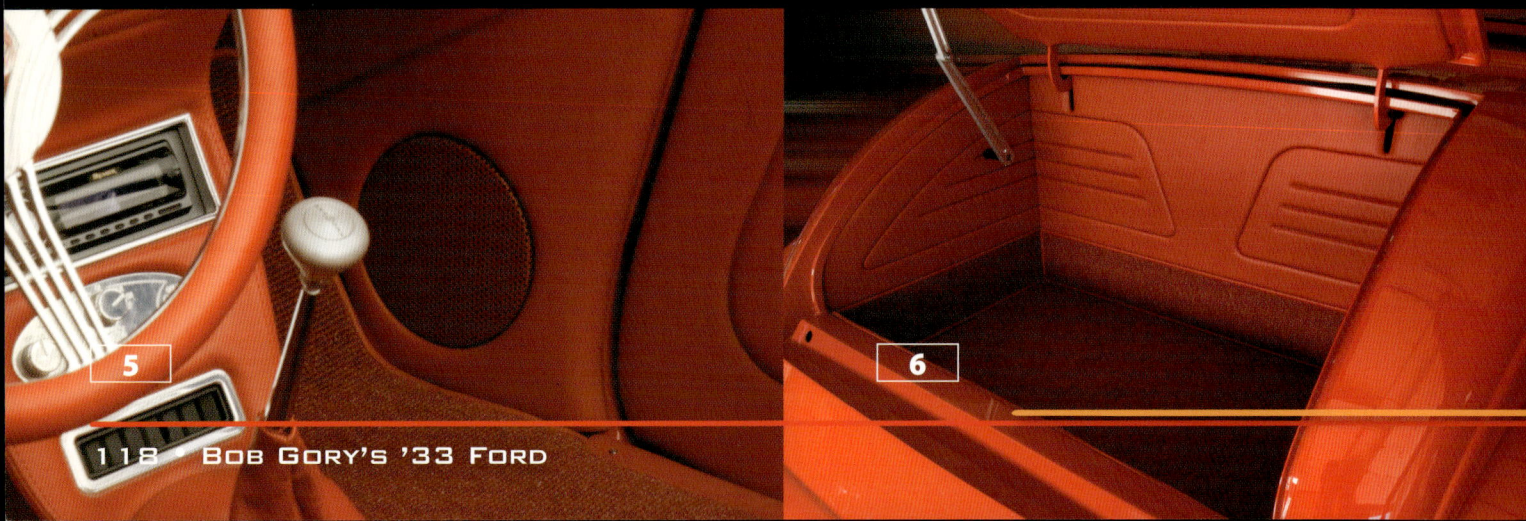

Ron Mangus' Custom Hot Rod Interiors • 119

JACK BOCKELMAN'S
'33 Ford Speedstar

Jack acquired his '33 Ford on a trade, but it turned out not to be everything he'd hoped for. The original Alloway chassis had been so poorly prepared by whoever first built the car that it couldn't be used, so another Alloway chassis was purchased and Jack completely rebuilt the car. McCabe Racing, Chino Valley, Arizona, welded chassis components, set up the drive train, and constructed the exhaust. During the rebuild, Jack also modified the body to include the head rest humps. The reconstruction took a year and a half, and was completed in November 2004.

Jack has known Ron Mangus for many years. So after the car was rebuilt, he took the car to Ron for a new interior, wanting a smooth and simple design. Ron's butter leather masterpiece features an organic design totally in character with the exaggerated stance of the car. This is the fourth interior Ron has done for Jack.

After they had enjoyed their rebuilt car a couple of years, Jack and his wife Connie saw a two-tone '33 at a car show, and approached Charles Armstrong to help them come up with a similar paint scheme for their car. Charles had to work around the completed interior, adding stunning metallic copper paint over the solid yellow transforming the car into a show stopper.

Body: Speedstar Roadster, Rat's Glass, Friendsville, Tennessee
Paint: Bob Sullivan, Chino Valley, Arizona, and
    Charles Armstrong, Auto Art, Prescott, Arizona (two-tone)
Engine: 350 Chevy
Drivetrain: 700R4 transmission, Heidt rear end,
Chassis: Alloway's Hot Rod Shop, Louisville, Tennessee,
    Heidt independent suspension
Wheels: Boze Speedster, front: 17", rear: 20"
Tires: BF Goodrich

Ron's interior design is very organic and blends with the flowing instrument panel shape that resolves at the back of the doors. Jack owned this car for several years before adding the copper two-tone paint.

Ron Mangus' Custom Hot Rod Interiors

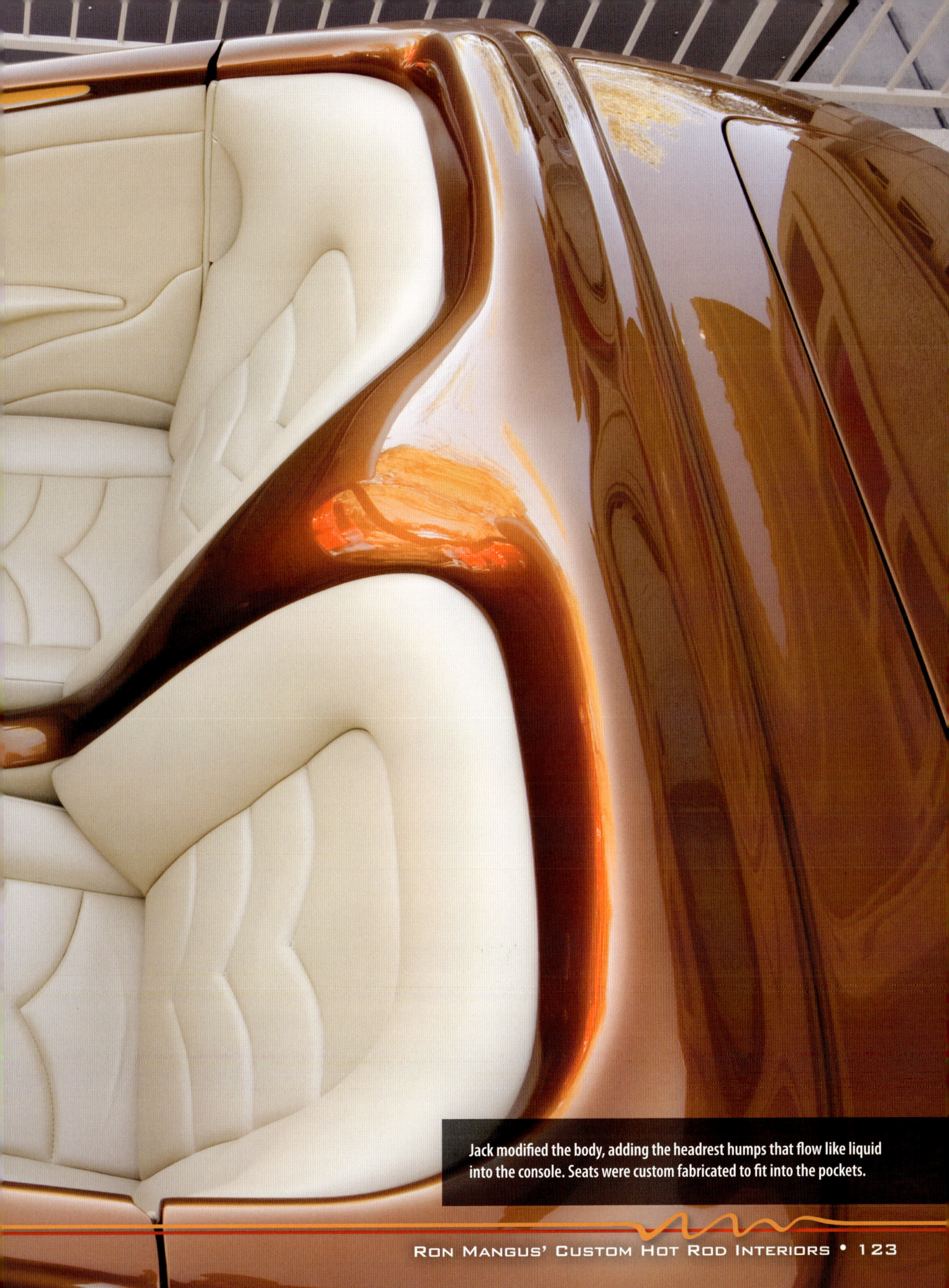

Jack modified the body, adding the headrest humps that flow like liquid into the console. Seats were custom fabricated to fit into the pockets.

1
The body flows into the console similar to that of '61–'62 Corvettes. The front of the seats have a large thigh bolster and a waterfall design.

2
Steering wheel is leather wrapped to add a finishing touch.

3
The front speakers are hidden behind sculpted kick panels featuring perforations instead of speaker grilles.

4
The car has a large column drop. Ron fabricated a cover that encloses the column so there is no column to instrument panel gap that would distract from the finished look of the interior.

5
This attention-getting shifter sports an oval chrome bezel and leather boot.

1
The seat shapes blend into the body, and carry the forms into the interior. It is as if there is a continuous form that comes into the interior changing materials at the tight gap between body and interior.

2
The seat design has a great deal of depth. The entire interior exhibits amazingly beautiful form control.

3
Special recesses located at the sides of the seats serve as sound openings for speakers that are mounted behind the seats.

4
The artistry of the flowing design is exemplified in the door panels.

5-6
The trunk is trimmed to match the interior, and the underside of the deck lid has a scalloped design. The fuel filler and the CD changer are on the back trunk panel.

7
The seating surfaces have an interesting gullwing-shaped design.

8
Jack's car has an aggressive stance. Let's check the engine, stash the gear, get in and go.

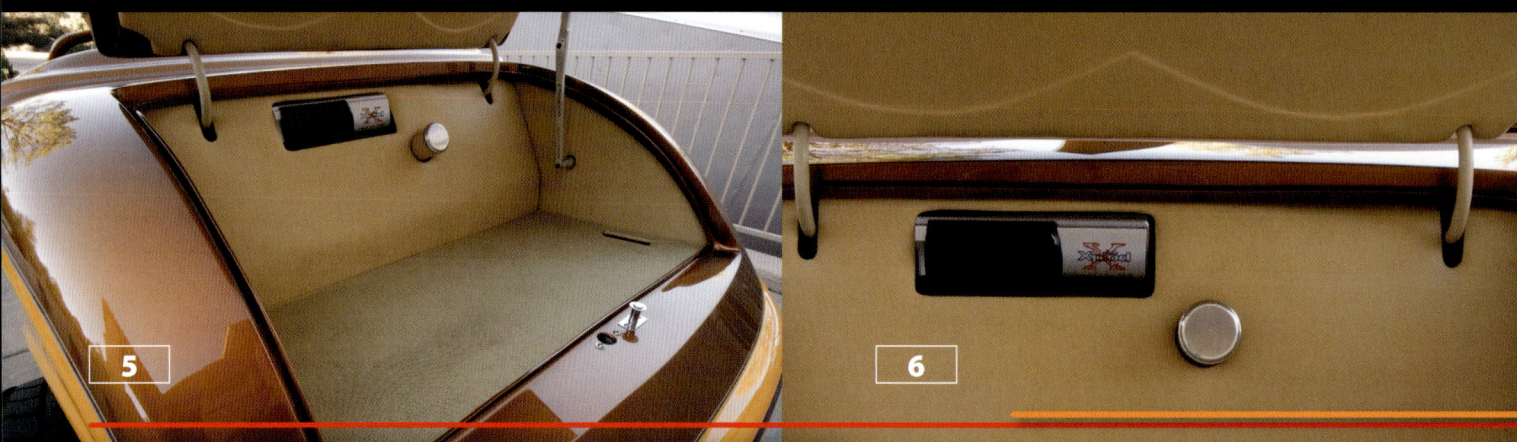

Ron Mangus' Custom Hot Rod Interiors • 127

KEN SAPPER'S
'32 Ford

Ken enjoyed a very successful 32-year racing career driving short track stock cars in the southwest as part of the promotion of his company, Speedway Engineering. Even though he didn't have to live from earnings, he was very competitive. For example, he won 27 features in the last three years of racing. He was nicknamed "Clark Kent" from his mild-mannered appearance, and competitors would put "Kryptonite" in the form of green rocks under his car to try and slow him down.

This '32 was originally built by Goldesberry Motorsports as a promotional car, and was displayed at SEMA. Speedway Engineering was one of the suppliers, and the car had one of their quick change rear ends. Ken saw the finished car at SEMA in 2003, and thought to himself that if he were to build a '32, it would be like this car. There was a small sticker on the car that read "available." Ken considered that, and approached Meryl Goldesberry. Ken realized that he couldn't buy the parts for what was being asked, and bought the car.

Ron tweaked the original interior for the Grand National Roadster Show, but at Ron's suggestion, Ken brought it back for some proper interior work. Especially important to Ken was comfort, and Ron was instrumental in upgrading the seating position and adding support where it was needed. Ken had a great experience working with Ron, recommends him, and would use him again.

Build by: Goldesberry Motorsports, Springfield, Illinois
Paint: Viper Red, by Goldesberry Motorsports, Springfield, Illinois
Engine: Chevy 350
Drivetrain: B&M TH-350, Super Max quick change rear end by
　　　　Speedway Engineering
Chassis: Heidt's Superride front suspension, QA1 Precision Products
　　　　coil overs
Wheels: Bon Speed Atomics, front: 17", rear: 20"
Tires: Toyo Proxes

After Ken bought the car, he took it to Ron for some minor interior work to get it ready for the Grand National Roadster Show in Pomona, California, and then later took the car back to Ron for an completely new interior.

1
The sides of interior have a sweeping design line that starts at the kick panels, runs through the doors, and loops around on the quarter panels. The low seat has a high thigh bolster and the back has plenty of lumbar support.

2
The seat back splits and folds down for gas tank access. The split was designed to coincide with the design of the seat, disguised as the upper design line of the seat back.

3
The shelf under the instrument panel is a great feature that Ron has used in many roadsters. It's a great place to place loose items that you need to bring with you.

4
Ron used German square-weave carpet. The shifter boot is leather with French stitching.

5
The firewall on Ken's roadster is leather.

1
The angled sculpted design in the quarter panels picks up the pattern from the seat.

2
Ken's roadster has a DuVall windshield, traditional instrument panel, and a nicely designed interior.

3
The doors have a very tight fit with no gaps. The straightforward "hard look" design fits the purposeful character of the car.

4
Seating surfaces are interrupted by this deeply sculpted and angled pattern.

5–6
Sculpted flat panels create interest without intruding into the interior space. The interior looks very spacious.

7–8
The trunk gets the same design treatment as the interior, with flat walls that have a flowing design.

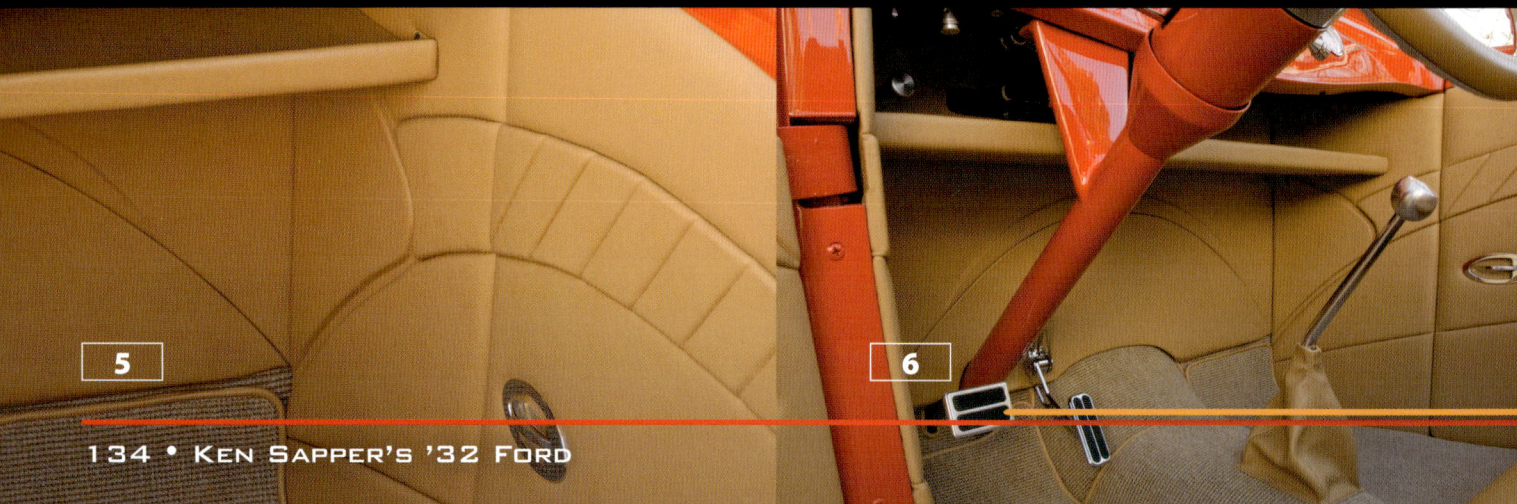

Ron Mangus' Custom Hot Rod Interiors • 135

CHICK KOSZIS'
'32 Ford

Chick's all-steel '32 has more than 40,000 miles on it. He has an album with photos showing the car in front of numerous national landmarks. In fact, after this photo shoot, Chick treated the photographer to an hour long, chilly December joyride around Valley Center, California. It was great. This car is *driven*.

The car has all kinds of interesting features. Check out the cast skeleton that resolves itself into paint and pinstripes on top of the head lamps. The matte black finish, pinstripes, skulls, louvers, raked windshield, stance, and blower all add up to a serious '32.

Ron's interior may be confined to the seat, but it's a good seat. The distressed leather is accented with custom embroidery patterned after the pinstriping on the deck lid. Chick is 6' 4" tall, so Ron designed the seat with a thigh bolster that is steeply angled, properly positioning Chick with ample legroom for extended comfort for his long trips. Pretty amazing considering the Deuce has a 5-inch chop! And in consideration of his wife, the seats have heated inserts to help take the chill off cold weather rides, and make the car a bit more civilized. Ron fit the top supplied by Dick Rodwell's Rodware, Salt Lake City, Utah.

Ron also was able to incorporate the skull graphics, taken from rubber floor mats, into his custom mats, as well as the "FTF" emblem that ended up over the transmission tunnel. The carpet, mats, and trunk are trimmed in dark gray German square-weave carpet.

Body: All steel by Rod Bods, Sparks, Nevada
Build and Paint: Hot Rods & Custom Stuff, Escondido, California
Pinstriping: Pete "Hot Dog" Finlan
Engine: 355 Chevy with 6-71 GMC Supercharger
Drivetrain: GM 700R4, Currie Ford 9-inch rear end
Chassis: SO-CAL Speed Shop
Wheels: 15" American Racing Torq-Thrust II

Chick explains what his roadster is all about: "I've always had a love of all things mechanical, including hot rods, custom cars, airplanes, and motorcycles. Hot rods hold the highest place in my own private, personal temple. Sue Ann and I were returning from a ten day motorcycle trip to northern California, and we were reflecting on the trip. She said that ten days on bikes was a bit much for her (she was riding her own Harley Fatboy). I replied that a roadster would have a lot of benefits over bikes: we could communicate a lot easier; we'd both make the same turns and get lost together; she could pack a curling iron if she wanted to, and the list went on. She agreed that a roadster would be pretty luxurious compared to a motorcycle. I took that vague acknowledgment of my brilliant analysis as tacit approval to build a roadster! The next day I called a friend, who I knew had a '32 roadster body for sale. A deal was struck and the birthing process began."

1
The seat is designed to accommodate Chick's tall frame. Ron used distressed leather, which is leather that has no protective coating. The more the seat is used, the more patina it develops. Red piping highlights the seating area.

2
The shift knob is a cast resin skull designed and produced by Dennis McPhail. This is the original knob that Pete Finlan "tattooed" when the car was initially built. Over the years it had acquired a worn look. Chick got another of the same casting, and had Pete tattoo that one also. It was "borrowed" from the car while parked at, of all places, the NHRA Museum. So the original knob is back on the car.

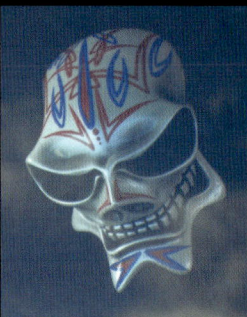

Photo by Chick Koszis

3–4
Chick found skull floor mats at Pep Boys, and brought them to Ron to have the skulls fit into Ron's custom mats.

5
The "FTF" emblem pretty much summarizes the whole disposition of the car.

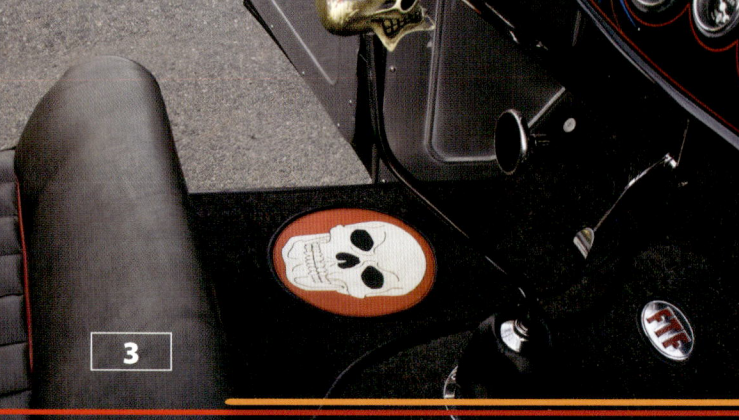

Ron Mangus' Custom Hot Rod Interiors • 141

1
Pete "Hot Dog" Finlan worked under the name Hot Dog Kustoms, and became well known pinstriping cars and motorcycles. He was working at Hot Rods & Custom Stuff when Chick built his '32. Chick wanted an old school look, and told him that the car was his canvas. Pete also created this pinstriping design that was embroidered on the seat.

2
Chick treated the photographer to a chilly morning ride around Valley Center, California.

3–4
The door panels are aluminum sheet with rolled bead stiffeners. They were fabricated at Hot Rods & Custom Stuff when the car was built. They are clear-coated to prevent corrosion—a good idea considering the car made a trip down the Bonneville salt flats.

5
Charlie and Stelle were Chick's parents.

6
Three-inch chopped, raked windshield and Rodwell top meant a lower seat had to be fabricated so Chick could again fit into his own car.

7
To maximize the available space in the trunk, Ron glued padding and carpet to the inside of the sheet metal.

8–9
The tilt wheel is made by Tri-C Engineering. Having the ability to change positions helps reduce fatigue on long drives.

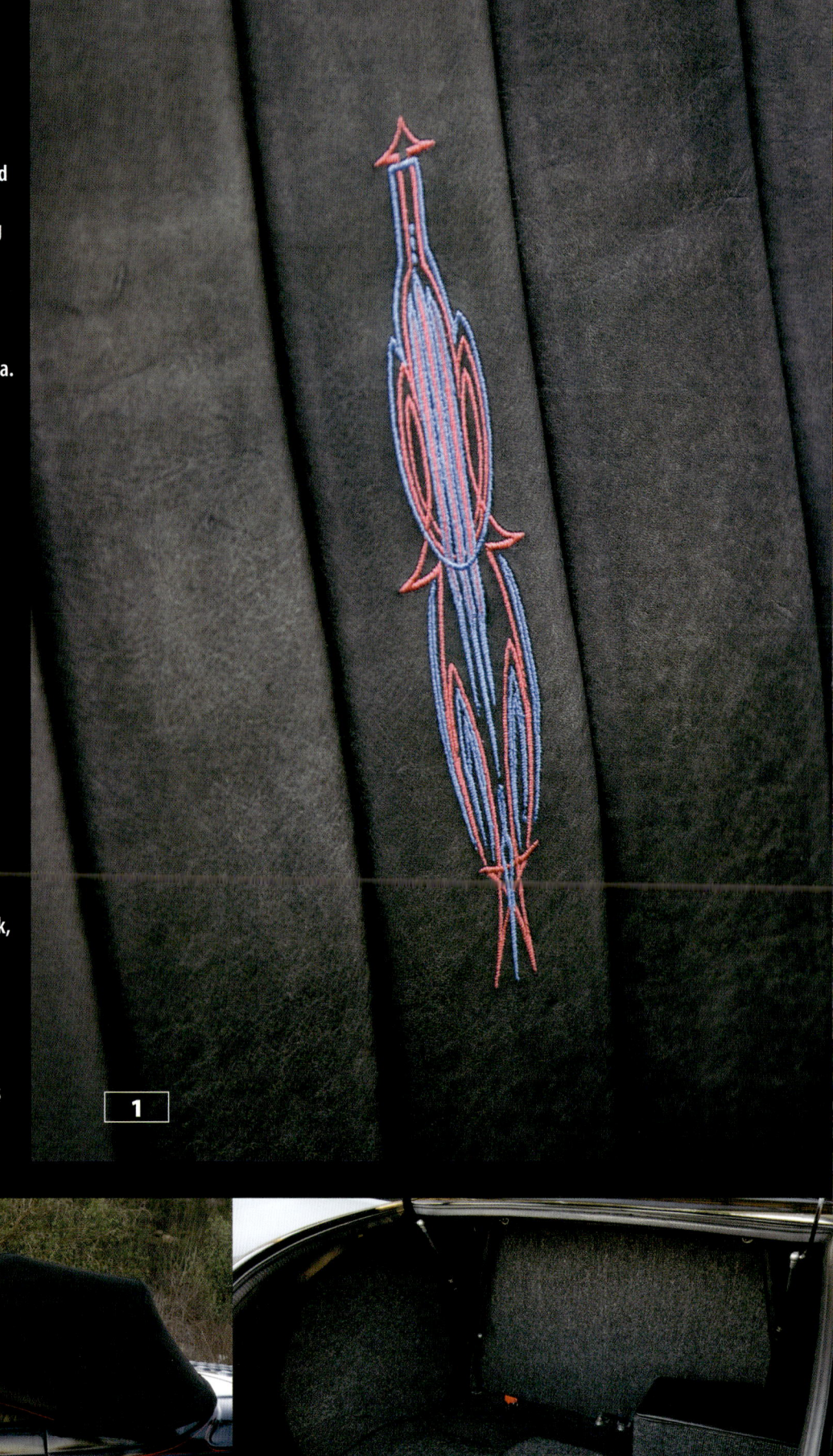

Photo by Chick Koszis

Ron Mangus' Custom Hot Rod Interiors • 143

FRED FLEET'S
'32 Ford

Fred's '32 is an extremely interesting car, and has many unique features uncharacteristic of contemporary hot rods, but completely consistent with the spirit of traditional hot rodding. The car is the first customer car built by SO-CAL, and has been featured in many European enthusiast magazines. The car was built in 1999, and updated many times since.

The Chevy 383 stroker motor has a handmade intake manifold that looks production, Hilborn electronic fuel injection, and custom billet valve covers. The wheels are a story all of their own. A collector needed wheels for his '50s era Watson Indianapolis 500 roadster he was restoring. Twenty sets were made, and this is one of those sets. The gold tint to the wheels is from the coating protecting the all-magnesium wheels. They have true knock-off hubs, anodized to match the finish of the wheels. The car was originally equipped with red wire wheels, so considerable modifications were made to accommodate the new mag wheels.

Fred went to Ron for upholstery, because that's where the first SO-CAL roadster was upholstered. Ron's brown leather interior has traditional styling, with many custom touches improving comfort and convenience, such as a folding center armrest, and kick panel storage pockets.

Body: All steel by Brookville Roadster, Inc., Brookville, Ohio
Build and Paint: SO-CAL Speed Shop, Pomona, California
Engine: Smeding built 475 hp, 383 Chevy stroker with handmade intake manifold featuring Hilborn fuel injection
Drivetrain: Richmond 5-speed
Chassis: SO-CAL Speed Shop, Pomona, California
Wheels: 16" one-piece magnesium "Kittyhawk" '50s era Watson Indy Roadster 6-pin drive wheels
Tires: Dunlop Racing, front: 5.50"×16", rear: 7.00"×18"

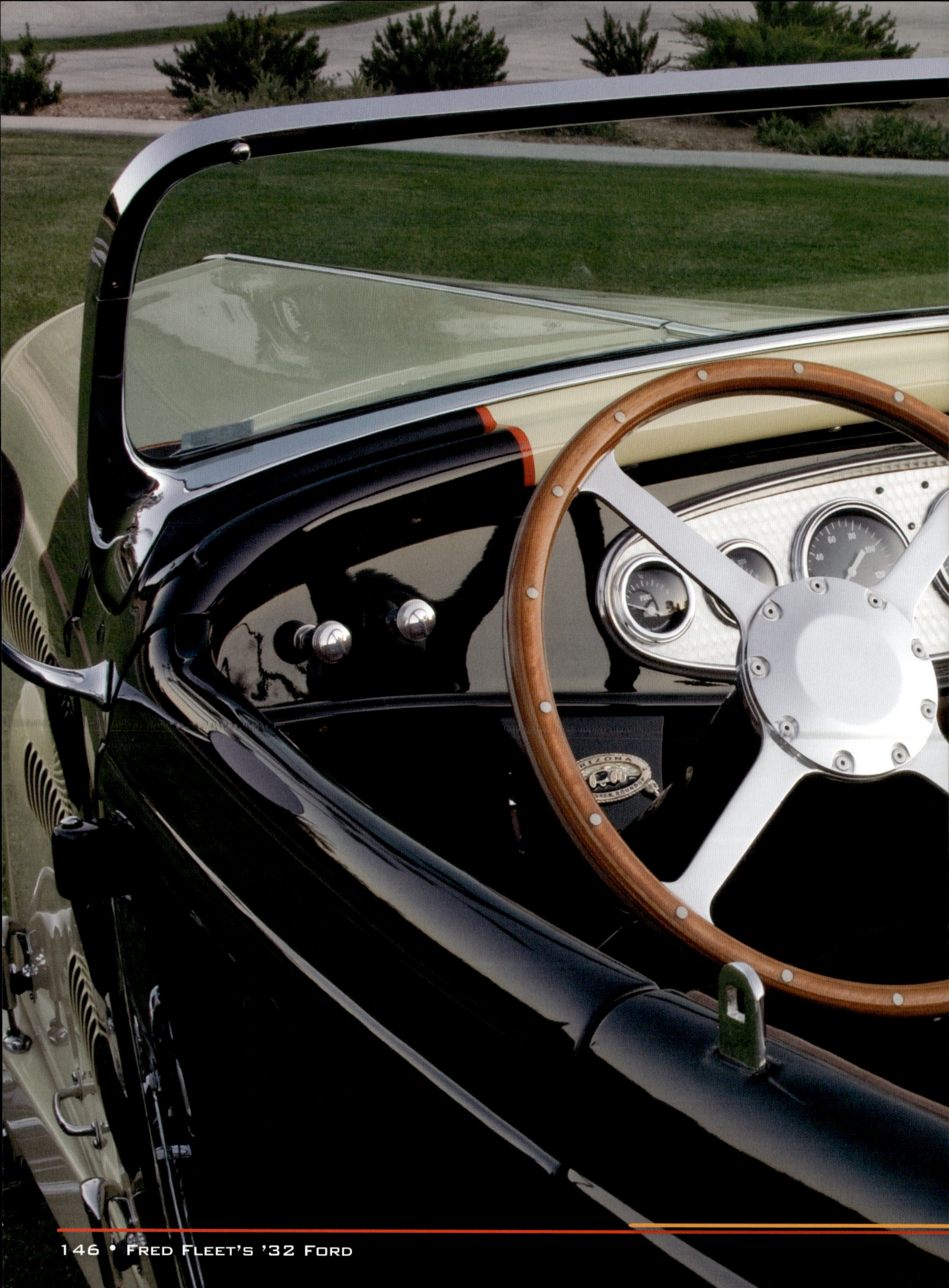

Fred used SO-CAL's two-tone paint scheme and had them paint the '32 with his colors, black and cream. He kept SO-CAL's traditional brown leather interior and added several custom touches that made the car his own.

Ron Mangus' Custom Hot Rod Interiors • 147

1
SO-CAL came up with a great '32 that started a revolution in the '90s towards traditional hot rodding. Fred's black and cream paint personalizes the car, but keeps the graphics that relate to the old-school SO-CAL paint scheme. The entire interior has a fitted luggage look to it.

2
Fred had a custom cloisonné emblem created from sterling silver.

3
The door panel has vertical tuck 'n roll pleats with matching piping. The door handle and bezel are the original '32 design.

4
Leather shifter boot is anchored to the floor with a bright trim ring.

5
On top of the shifter is a cool metal skull shift knob, cast by Adam Weisman of Phoenix.

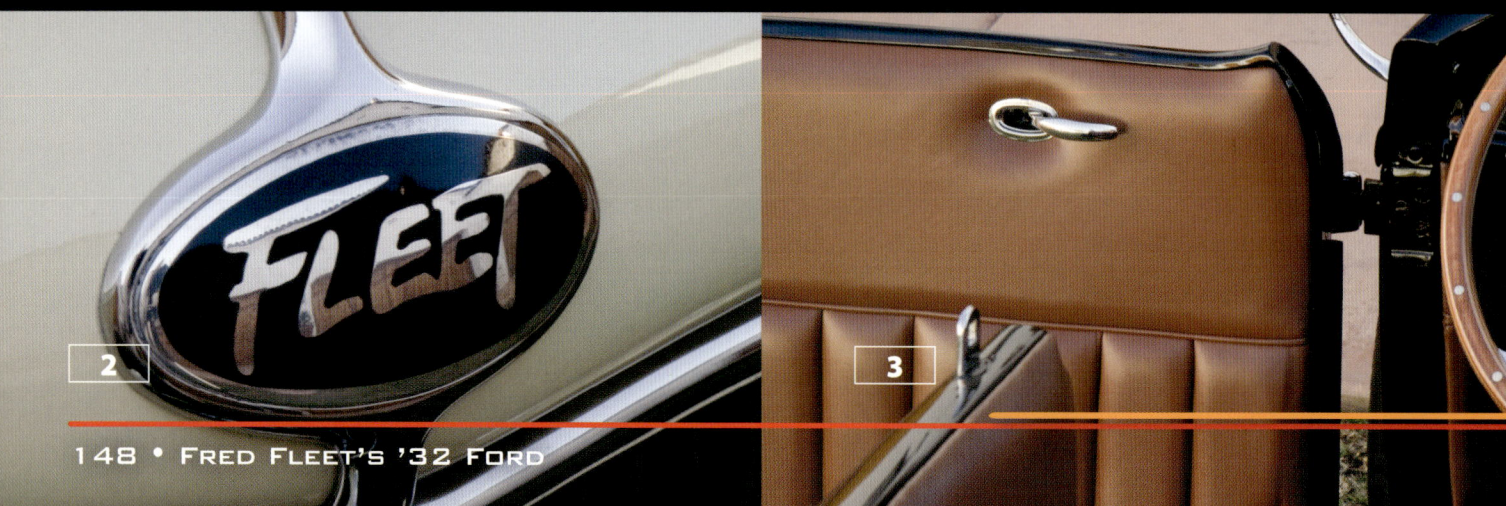

1
Glide Engineering makes a versatile seat frame that allows a great deal of adjustment, including a reclining feature.

2
Vertical pleats characterize the old-school feel of the interior. The front of the seat has an ample thigh bolster that helps cradle the occupants and keeps them in the seat.

3
The wheels are cast magnesium reproductions of '50s era Watson Indy car roadster racing wheels.

4
Fred ordered the Glide seat with a flip down armrest. The profile of the armrest matches the lumbar put into the seat for comfort.

5
There are custom leather pockets built into the kick panels to store loose items.

6
The car doesn't have air conditioning, but it does have a heater to take the chill off of cold morning drives. Ron enclosed the heater box with a custom cover.

7
The car has a five-speed manual transmission, and the floor surrounding the shifter is nicely tailored in German square-weave carpet with leather edging.

8
The trunk has padding and carpet glued directly to the inside of the body to maximize trunk space.

MAC BERND'S
'32 Ford

Mac has been a hot rodder for years, adopting a long list of cars in various stages of development and turning them into show pieces. The problem with that is coping with the frustration of having to try and remedy poorly executed details or component placement that may be cost prohibitive, difficult, or impossible to effectively fix.

This car, however, was built from the ground up, and Mac engineered the locations and configurations of components so they are conveniently and practically located. For example, instead of having to stand on your head to replace a fuse that is under the dash, the fuse box is easily accessible under a cover in the trunk.

The car also features a convertible top concealed with a steel body panel supplied by Dearborn Deuce.

Mac and his wife Shelley wanted a beautiful, understated roadster with a '30s high-end European sports-luxury car look. Their '32 definitely combines a contemporary flare and retro details, with a hot rod attitude.

Body: All-steel Dearborn Deuce
Build and Paint: The Roadster Shop, Mundelein, Illinois (rolling chassis, body modifications), and Randy Borcherding, Painthouse, Tomball, Texas (disassembly, gap corrections, body modifications, paint: Red Hot Meltdown by Hot Hues)
Engine: Chevy ZZ430, Street & Performance, Mena, Arkansas; Tuning by Extreme Automotive, Corona, California
Drivetrain: Tremec TKO 600, Ford 9-inch rear end
Chassis: The Roadster Shop, Mundelein, Illinois
Wheels: Budnik Muroc II, front: 17"×6", rear: 20"×10"
Tires: Toyo, front: 205/40×17", rear: 275/40×20"

Photos by Shelley Bernd / HotRodHappenings.com

Ron has upholstered three cars for Mac and Shelley. They gave him a vision of what they had in mind using several interior concept renderings by Eric Brockmeyer, and they relied on Ron's artistic judgment. Sometimes hot rod design themes have a short life span because the designs reflect popular styling typical at the time the car was built, or they are so outlandish that the design grows tiresome. What Mac and Shelley wanted was to create a timeless classic that is reminiscent of the art deco elegance found in Duesenbergs and other classics of the '30s. With Ron's input, their vision evolved into this classic show car.

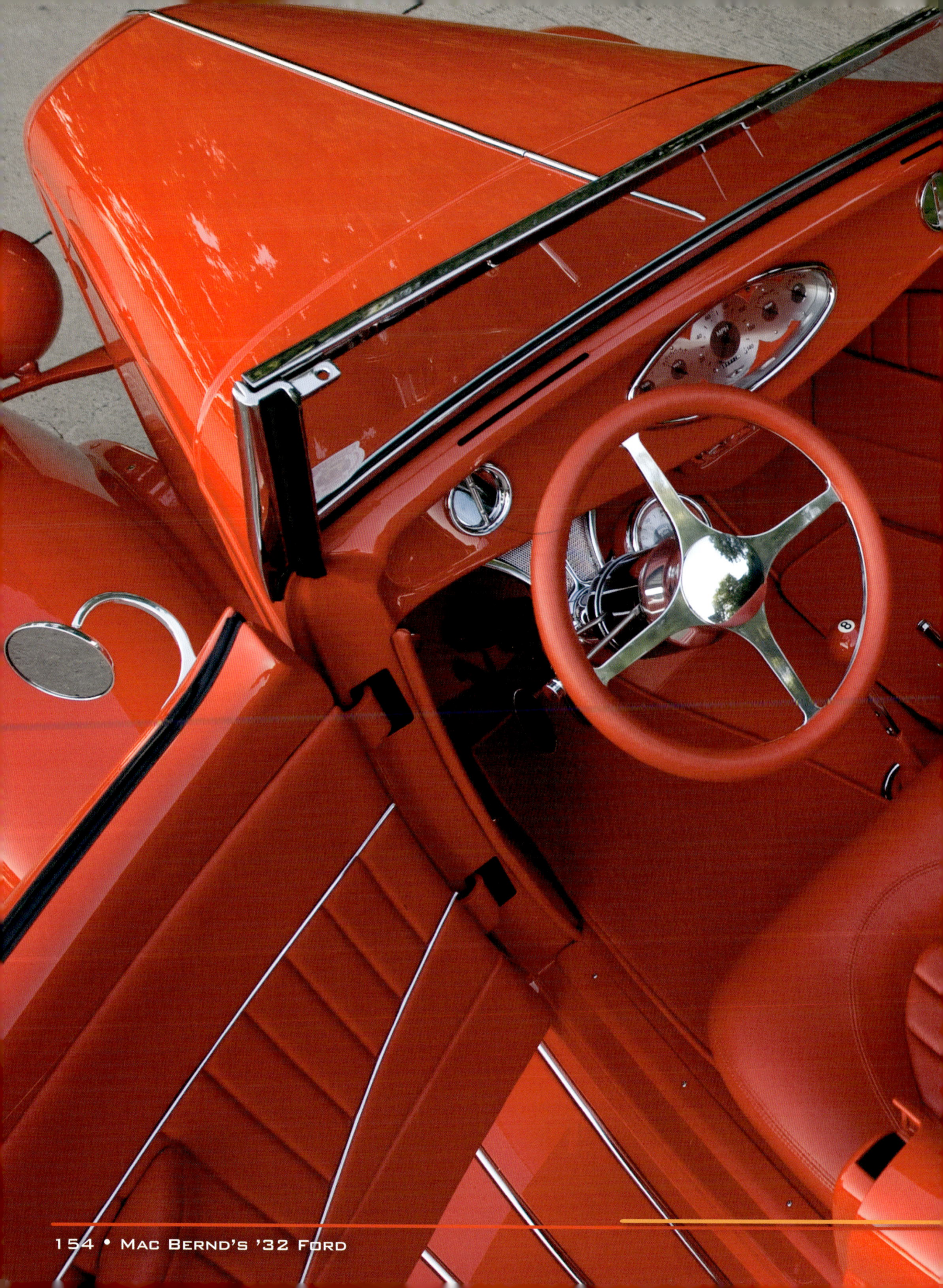

Three chrome strips on the running boards and inlaid, custom chrome trim on the sides of the interior convey the classic retro styling of this '32. The seating areas, doors, kick panels, and quarter panels all have the same pleated leather design. Elliptical shapes define the interior theme.

1
Unique elliptically shaped seating areas with French stitched accent lines have a classic retro look. A closer inspection reveals that comfort was not sacrificed for styling. The seats have ample side bolster and lumbar support. The inlaid chrome trim on the upper section of the quarter panels stops short and allows the last pleat to blend into the upper part of the panel.

2
The elliptical theme begins with inlaid chrome on the kick panels.

3
The custom red eight ball shifter is trimmed in a leather boot and secured with a chrome trim ring. Too cool.

4
The armrest has nicely sculpted, classic shape with inlaid chrome used as an accent.

5
The transmission tunnel is covered in leather with carpeted foot wells and custom floor mats.

Ron Mangus' Custom Hot Rod Interiors • 157

1
The convertible top folds down into this compartment and is hidden by a flush-mounted metal body panel.

2
The theme brings the chrome molding detail from the running boards into the interior. Straight door pleats and classic armrests are set off by inlaid chrome—true retro.

3
Budnick Turn 4 steering wheel has classic track racing styling. All of the individual interior elements come together in perfect harmony.

4
Elliptical pedals carry on the interior theme.

5–6
The elliptical interior theme begins with inlaid chrome on the kick panels, continues through the doors, and finishes on the quarter panels.

7–8
The vertically pleated leather surrounded by inlaid chrome trim is repeated in the trunk, finishing the design theme of the car.

Ron Mangus' Custom Hot Rod Interiors • 159

Thanks to our friends:

Acme Auto Headlining Co.
550 W. 16th St.
Long Beach, CA 90813
800-288-6078
www.acmeautoheadlining.com

Auto Custom Carpets, Inc.
P.O. Box 1350
1429 Noble St.
Anniston, AL 36202
800-352-8216
www.accmats.com

B & M Foam & Fabrics
3383 Durahart St.
Riverside, CA 92507
951-787-0221

Cerullo Performance Seating
2881 Metropolitan Place
Pomona, CA 91767
909-392-5561
www.cerullo.com

Extreme Automotive
18889 Grovewood Dr.
Corona, CA 92881
951-371-9730
www.extremeautomotive.org

Garrett Leather
(trade only)
1360 Niagara St.
Buffalo, NY 14213
800-342-7738
www.garrettleather.com

Glide Engineering, Inc.
10662 Pullman Ct.
Rancho Cucamonga, CA 91730
800-301-3334
www.glideeng.com

J & J Auto Fabrics, Inc.
247 S. Riverside Ave.
Rialto, CA 92376
909-874-3040
www.jjautofabrics.com

Keyston Bros.
(nationwide wholesale only)
1833 Riverview Dr., Ste. B
San Bernardino, CA 92408
909-796-5391
www.keystonbros.com

LeBaron Bonney
P.O. Box 6
6 Chestnut St.
Amesbury, MA 01913
800-221-5408
www.lebaronbonney.com

Original Parts Group
1770 Saturn Way
Seal Beach, CA 90740
800-243-8355
www.opgi.com

Quality Heat Shield
555 N. Main St.
Riverside, CA 92501
951-788-2903

Robbins Auto Tops
321 Todd Ct.
Oxnard, CA 93030
805-604-3200
www.robbinsautotopco.com

Ron Mangus Hot Rod Interiors
247 S. Olive Ave.
Rialto, CA 92376
909-877-9342
www.ronmangusinteriors.com

Tea's Design
2038 15th St. NW
Rochester, MN 55901
800-791-7328
www.teasdesign.com

The Truck Stop
dba Specialty Conversions
1889 W. Commonwealth Ave.
Fullerton, CA 92833
714-870-7920
www.buckle-up.net

Veteran Company
(wholesale only)
5060 W. Pico Blvd.
Los Angeles, CA 90019
800-524-3330
www.veteranco.com